20

SIMPLE LETTERS,

PERFECTLY FORMED

- BY -

KAREN S. BARBERA

Printed in the United States of America.

Library of Congress Control Number: 2023946619

ISBN   Paperback   979-8-88887-701-2
              eBook   979-8-88887-702-9

Westwood Books Publishing LLC
Atlanta Financial Center
3343 Peachtree Rd NE Ste 145-725
Atlanta, GA 30326

www.westwoodbookspublishing.com

This book is dedicated to "Shorty" and all immigrants for their bravery, perseverance, hard work and self-sacrifice, so their families could build better lives.

DAUGHTERS
Angie, Joanne and Christina

GRANDCHILDREN
Carol, Karen, George, Beth, Jim and Pano

GREAT GRANDCHILDREN
Christy, Andrew, Audrey, Calvin, Cameron, Abigail, Avery, Chandler, John, Paul, Eleni, Johnny, Carey and Eleni

GREAT, GREAT GRANDCHILDREN
Annabelle, Jack, Atlas, Eleni, Poesy, Cimeon, Salix, Everette, Ruby, Brooklyn, Esme, Charlotte Jo and...

LEST WE FORGET

The monumental building,
flag fluttering atop,
commands our attention and awe;

The bedrock and underpinnings
from which it springs
remain hidden and unremarkable.

Lest we forget,
the world's greatest achievements
are built upon the selfless acts of
everyday people.

Karen Barbera

CONTENTS

LAFKA, GREECE 1911-1919

Looking back on my childhood...I realize how small and simple my world of understanding was. At nine years of age, I didn't know much beyond my own basic needs and my absolute trust and love for my family. I didn't realize that we were very poor. I didn't understand the burden of raising six daughters in a country where life revolved entirely around males, sons in particular. And I certainly had no way of knowing how my simplest, yet proudest accomplishment would alter the course of my life.

I lived in the small village of Lafka, high in the mountains of Greece, where it was traditional for multiple generations of a single family to live together under one roof; for marriages to be arranged; for the oldest son to inherit the family home and meager land holdings; for the matriarch to give up her status as the head of her own household to her oldest son's wife; and for younger sons to marry and start their own families in nearby homes of their own, yet continue to work the family's land. I understand now, that while daughters were considered a gift from God, they were also a financial burden, requiring costly dowries for their arranged marriages.

My childhood experiences continued as they had for centuries in my country. With the birth of each new generation, newly minted *Yia-Yia's* and *Papou's* (grandmothers and grandfathers) were retired to supporting roles, tending grandchildren and household chores, mending tools in need of repair, and performing less physical forms of labor while the younger, more vigorous members of the household shepherded small herds of goats and sheep, or toiled shoulder-to-shoulder with extended relatives in the family's checkerboard plots of currants, grapevines, vegetables and groves of olive, nut and fruit trees.

It wasn't until I was older that I realized just how resilient and hardworking we were; how few possessions were truly needed and how resources of every kind could be used and reused to exhaustion. Excess and waste were luxuries few Greek families could afford.

Each fall, we carefully bundled the trimmings from our grape vines and orchards with twine and stacked them against the chicken coop to later fuel our cooking fires, heat wash water and warm our one-room home. We even coveted the resulting fire ash, depositing it in a nearby pit where it would miraculously transform, over time and with the addition of water, into a thick, brilliantly white lye that we used to make soap and whitewash the stone walls of our house and outbuildings.

Harvested foods we couldn't immediately consume were meticulously preserved. Grapes were dried by the sun into raisins. Currants and fruits were dried or preserved with honey in containers sealed with melted bee's wax. Olives were pressed for cooking oil, or cured in heavily brined water to remove the bitterness and preserve them. Nuts and root vegetables were stored in cool caves or underground cellars. And the milk from our goats was made into *tyri* (cheese): soft *feta* and hard *mijethra*.

We grazed our sheep, goats and donkeys on the rocky, mountainside behind our home and drove them down to a watering hole twice a day in return for their life-sustaining wool, milk, meat and transportation. It was a hard, yet simple life with complex lessons that created strong family bonds and an inner strength that would comfort me in the lonely hours that laid ahead.

-Panagiota Athanasouli

GREECE

In the late 1800's, most extended Greek families lived a strictly agrarian lifestyle, raising whatever animals and foodstuffs they could grow on their land in their dry, Mediterranean climate. When the Turks invaded Greece in 1897, during the Greco-Turkish War, all able-bodied men were conscripted from their farms to the battlefields to defend their country and preserve their culture. When they returned, sometimes crippled, many ripped out their grape vines and fruit trees to plant the more lucrative crop of currants which were in high demand by France. Families and villages prospered for several years until the French imposed staggering import taxes, collapsing the market in Greece…as well as most hard working families' hopes for prosperity.

The ensuing decades were filled with hardships, and the country, and its people suffered greatly. Large, extended families did their best to work their fields, but as the market for their crops dwindled, they experienced severe poverty. It was not uncommon for families to send daughters to Athens to become housemaids. They weren't paid much, but at least they were housed and fed. Other extended family members immigrated to Australia or America in search of better opportunities and lives. These brave emissaries banded together in far-flung foreign places, looking after one another and sharing whatever resources were available.

Immigrating To America

The Athanasouli family lived in the small village of Lafka, Greece. Athanasios (Thanasi) was the eldest of four sons born to Athanasios (Sr.) and Pelagia Athanasouli in 1882. He and his brothers Panagiotis (Paul), Kostantinos (Kosta) and Georgios, (George) struggled to support their family, working the land and selling crops in the village marketplace. When Thanasi married Kostandia Barbopoulos in 1905, his wife's meager dowry provided short term relief, but the addition of their baby daughter Xeni and the prospect of additional children strained the family's resources. One year later, at the age of twenty-four, Thanasi and his two younger brothers, Panagiotis (21) and Kosta (20), sold what surplus goods they could and booked passage on a ship destined for America. Thanasi's young wife Konstandina stayed behind with her in-laws and brother-in-law Georgios (15) to tend the family crops and scratch out a life of subsistence as baby Xeni grew into a toddler.

Immigrating to America during this time period required proof of family or friends living in America who were willing to sponsor and house new arrivals until they could become self-supporting. The bothers' *Theo* (uncle) Mitsio Skiza, who had been in the United States long enough to establish a shoe shine shop in Newark, Ohio, provided the necessary paperwork and lodging. When the three Athanasouli brothers arrived, they joined their uncle and his son Georgios (George), living in their one-room apartment above the shop and quickly Americanized their last name to the less-ethnic-sounding *Athan*.

After several weeks acclimating to their new country, Thanasi, Panagiotis and Kosta used their *Theo's* shoe shine shop as a springboard to secure jobs laying railroad tracks. It was well paying but physical work under primitive conditions. They worked year 'round through the cold winters, sleeping in empty boxcars, so they could send as much money as possible back to their struggling families in Greece. A few years later, they sent a prepaid ticket for their youngest brother Georgios to join them. He arrived, but fell ill, necessitating a hasty return to Greece to be nursed back to health by Thanasi's wife Kostandina. When he regained his strength, he returned to America; not to the railroads this time, but to Theo

Mitosis Skiza's shoe shine shop where he and his cousin Georgios Skiza took over the running of the shoe shine shop, allowing the older Skiza to return to Greece and retire.

Unfortunately, illness struck again, claiming the life of Mitsio's son Georgios. Out of respect for all that the Skiza family had done for the Athanasouli family, Georgios Athan (Athanasoulis) paid for his cousin's funeral and made sure he was properly laid to rest. Then, he closed the shoe shine shop, and along with Harry and Sam Athan, two additional cousins who also immigrated from a nearby Greek village, moved to the smaller, more affordable town of Shelby, Ohio. There, the three relatives pooled their savings and purchased the Elite Restaurant, renaming it the Crystal Restaurant.

While Thanasi was in America, his wife Kostandina and her husband's family "made due" back in Greece as baby Xeni grew into a toddler. When her husband returned four years later, he used his American earnings to build a much needed flour mill in their village, fulfilling his dream to create a more prosperous life for his family. Ten months later, Thanasi and Kostandia welcomed their second daughter, naming her Panagiota (Pauline) after Thanasi's brother Panagiotis.

When Panagiota grew up, Kostandina told her daughter, "It was very difficult and lonely while your *Baba* (father) was away, but when he returned from America, he brought me *you* as a special gift!" Her mother's simplified story made Panagiota feel special. It also explained why her sister Xeni was five years older than her... and so used to getting her way.

THE ATHANASOULIS FAMILY

Lafka, Greece - 1920

The penetrating rasps of roosters interrupt the morning's stillness, moving slowly down the mountain in tandem with the emerging morning light. Eight-year-old Panagiota keeps still in her bed, but her eyes are open. Her thirteen year-old-old sister Xeni rolls over, pulling the blanket off of her and her seven-year-old younger sister Dimetra, but it is a relief this time. It is early Spring. The rekindled fire has made it warm inside the house, and Panagiota has a sheen of sweat on her brow. She watches her *Baba* (father) button his vest over his shirt as he pushes the wooden shutter aside for a glimpse at the new morning light and a breath of crisp spring air.

Panagiota opens and closes her small hands, wondering if Xeni's and Dimitra's are as chapped and sore. The three sisters spent the last two days helping their *Mama* air out the house after the long, stuffy winter, washing their clothes and bed linens in the stone basin outside. Lye and boiling water helped clean the roughly woven fabrics, but the harsh combination dried and burned the sisters' skin as they scrubbed the bulky fabrics up and down against the side of the chiseled stone; their arms sore from scrubbing, their shoulders stiff from carrying buckets of water from the well to the fire to be heated.

Panagiota watches as her *Mama* returns quietly to the house with two wooden buckets of well water, setting them gently on the stone ledge between the window and the hearth. Behind her on the sturdy kitchen table, she has already set out the family's breakfast: olives, *feta* cheese, hard boiled eggs and some bread. The sight of the water and food make Panagiota realize how thirsty and hungry she is. Her stomach growls.

She sees her *Baba* touch her *Mama's* arm as if to comfort or console her as he speaks earnestly to her in hushed tones. Just then, Panagiota's younger sister Tasia sneezes, and baby Olga stirs in her cradle. Her parents still for a moment, anticipating the baby's wail, but she quiets. Panagiota sees them relax a bit, but the anguished look on her *Mama's* face returns as *Baba* continues his whispers.

Moments later, Tasia sits up in her parent's bed. She is three-years-old and wide awake. Her *Mama* glances at Tasia then quickly over her shoulder at her three older daughters in their communal bed. Panagiota closes her eyes quickly, so her mother won't see she is awake, but she isn't fast enough.

"Παναγιώτα!" Her *Mama* whispers urgently. *"Πάρτε την Tasia στο μπάνιο. Γρήγορα! Πριν βρέξει το κρεβάτι!* (Panagiota! Take Tasia to the bathroom. Quick! Before she wets the bed!)"

Panagiota scrambles carefully away from Xeni and over Dimitra onto the hard packed dirt floor. It feels cool and comforting to her bare feet as she pads over and pulls Tasia from her parents' bed.

"Έλα εδώ, Τασία, (Come here, Tasia)," Panagiota coos softly to her little sister. Tasia is old enough to walk, but she clings sleepily to her older sister.

As Panagiota carries her to the door, their *Mama* drapes a worn, woolen shawl around their shoulders. *"Kánei krýo éxo!* (It's cold outside)," their *Mama* says. *"Káne grígora!"* (Be quick!)"

Panagiota balances Tasia on her left hip, leaning awkwardly to her right to help counterbalance her weight as she staggers out the door toward the whitewashed outhouse a short distance from the house. Panagiota is strong, but her sister Tasia is more than half her size and heavy.

"Καλημέρα (Good morning)," Panagiota says softly against Tasia's ear. *"Σε πηγαίνω στο γιογιό* (I am taking you to the potty)." *"Κοιτάξτε πόσο όμορφο είναι σήμερα!* (Look how beautiful it is today!)" *"Koimíthikes kalá?* (Did you sleep okay?)" The toddler nods her head shyly against her sister's neck.

They pass the chicken coop and hear the familiar clucking of hens. It is Panagiota's job to collect the freshly-laid eggs each morning, and she absently wonders how many she will find this morning. It's one of her favorite chores…like gathering presents. Her *Baba* keeps the rooster away from the hens by tying a short length of twine around his leg, securing the other end to a wooden stake driven into the ground just outside the hen house where he can still walk, strut and crow. But sometimes the rooster wiggles loose, and her *Baba* tells her she can't gather the eggs for a few days. He helps her carefully mark these *rooster eggs* which the hens are allowed to warm with their bodies until they hatch into new baby chicks. It means the family will go without eggs for a couple of days, but when the hatchlings are grown, the family will be able to butcher a mature chicken and enjoy meat at one of their meals. This is a very special treat even to think about, and Panagiota's stomach growls, again, in anticipation.

Suddenly, Tasia cries out, *"Γρήγορα, Παναγιώτα! Πρέπει να πάω τουαλέτα!* (Hurry, Panagiota! I have to go potty!)"

Panagiota throws off their shawl and bursts through the outhouse door. She lifts her sister's simple night shift and tries to position Tashia's feet on either side of the single hole in the dirt floor. She supports her little sister around her waist, clenching the fabric of her night gown in one hand while fumbling with her other to slide Tasia's other foot awkwardly to the right.

"Κάτσε κάτω, Τασία!, (Squat down, Tasia!)" She says urgently with a bit of frustration. Tasia does her best, but not before urine starts to run down her leg…and her sister's hand.

"Να χαθείς! (Loosely translated as 'Go disappear!')" Panagiota mutters under her breath, something she has heard her *Baba* and *Mama* say in times of crisis. The tone of her outburst hurts Tasia's feelings, and she begins to cry.

"Δεν πειράζει! Είναι εντάξει! (It's okay! It's okay!)" Panagiota reassures her.

Finally, they achieve success as the urine stream comes out with more force and reaches its appropriate target. Panagiota shakes the wetness from her free hand and balances Tasia until she is finished.

"*Ορίστε, Tasia!* (There we go, Tasia!)" She says, trying to cheer her little sister. "*Βλέπουμε, το καταλάβαμε!* (See, we figured it out!)" Tasia smiles reluctantly and squeezes her sister's neck as she tries to climb back into her arms.

"*Περίμενε ένα λεπτό! Περίμενε ένα λεπτό!* (Wait a minute! Wait a minute!)," Panagiota says as she disentangles herself from her sister's grip. "*Κι εγώ πρέπει να πάω στην τουαλέτα!* (I have to go too!)"

When she is done, Panagiota steps up on a large stone against the back wall, stretching onto her toes to reach the spigot of the metal watering can suspended on a high hook. It is filled each day with well water for bathing, but this morning she uses handfuls to rinse the urine from her hands and Tasia's legs.

"*Στεγνώστε τον εαυτό σας με το νυχτικό σας, Tasia* (Dry yourself with your nightshirt, Tasia)," she tells her little sister as she does the same.

When they are finished, Panagiota lifts Tasia back onto her hip, kisses her cheek and awkwardly twirls the warm shawl around their shoulders. The sun's rays are just peeking over the mountain tops. Tendrils of aromas from fresh baked bread and wood smoke waft seductively into the air from the surrounding village. They slip quickly back into the warmth and clamor of their stacked-stone home, as their family readies itself for another day of physically demanding work.

"*Καλημέρα κυρίες!* (Good morning, ladies!)" Their *Baba* says as he slides past his daughters on his way out the same door they just entered. He cradles Panagiota's cheek with his rough, calloused hand and kisses Tasia on the head as he glances back at Kostandina. "*Ο Γιάννης είναι εδώ νωρίς με την τσάντα του με τα σιτηρά.*" (John is here early with his bag of grain), he says, explaining his hasty departure[1].

But John will have to wait for his flour to be ground while Thansi readies the mill and harnesses the donkeys to the stout wooden lever that turns the heavy grinding stone. Like most years at this time, much of the harvested wheat has already been consumed over the winter. Food stores among the villagers are low, and many families are

---

1 All future dialogue will continue in English only for ease of reading.

only able to pay Thanasi Athanasoulis with what few goods remain: animals, nuts, root vegetables, currants, eggs, or a small portion of their ground flour. He feels badly accepting their offerings, but has little choice if he wants to feed his own family of seven.

Back in their home, Kostandina sets her daughters' day in motion as she changes a fussy Olga's diaper. Their Spring cleaning will continue after breakfast as their *Baba* works in the mill. The three oldest girls begin by carrying the heavy woven rugs outside to drape them over tree limbs and bushes, so a winter's worth of dirt can be drubbed out of them with large sticks.

"Xeni," *Mama* says, stopping her oldest daughter, "Take your sisters outside while I nurse Olga and Tashia finishes eating. I'll need you to help them with the rugs while I prepare our afternoon meal."

Panagiota and Dimetra exchange a knowing glance. They are old enough to beat the rugs and whitewash the house with a little help, which means that while *Mama* cooks and nurses the baby, they will be bossed around by their older sister. *Mama* is very protective of Olga. She is almost one year old, the same age as their brother Spiro when he died four years ago.

"Panagiota and Dimetra!" Barks Xeni, true to her sisters' expectations. "Take these rugs outside while I gather the beating sticks for you."

"Always the easiest job for her," Dimitra mutters uncharitably under her breath. Panagiota elbows Dimitra and imitates the superior look on Xeni's face. The girls laugh as they gather up the first rug and drag it toward the door. The effort reacquaints both girls with the soreness in their hands and shoulders, but Panagiota doesn't really mind. The heavy rugs were woven by their *YiaYia* (grandmother) many years ago on a large wooden loom, using shuttles of hand dyed wool yarns from the family's sheep. And she enjoys being out in the sunshine, doing physical work.

Xeni arrives with Tasia in one hand and the beating sticks in the other just in time to help her two younger sisters heft the first rug over the horizontal branch of a squatty lemon tree. Panagiota and Dimetra stand on opposite sides of the rug and set up an alternating rhythm with their large sticks.

"You're getting stronger, Panagiota," Xeni observes, looking on with a smile on her face as she sits with Tasia. "You'll be able to help *Baba* in the mill pretty soon."

Panagiota savors the rare compliment and tries not to wait for the dropping of the other proverbial *papoutsi* (shoe).

"Dimetra," continues Xeni, "You're old enough now to help *Mama* in the house and with baby Olga. Would you like that?"

"It's going to be a busy year," continues Xeni smugly as if she knows something her sisters don't.

Dimetra and Panagiota exchange a questioning glance.

"*Baba* told me this morning he wants me to work harder on my letters and writing," Xeni says, affecting a tone of nonchalance.

Panagiota senses that Xeni enjoys being singled out and having an excuse to escape her chores, but that she isn't *thrilled* about having them replaced with school work. The three oldest sisters attend school in the village when time permits. Although Panagiota is five years younger than Xeni, she is farther along with her lettering and writing. In Xeni's defense, she is needed more often by her mother, and recently, distracted by thoughts of which young man her parents will choose for her as she approaches marrying age.

In the male-dominate Greek culture, only sons can inherit property and bring wealth to their own families through marital dowries. Daughters can only better themselves -- and lessen their burden on their families -- by marrying and becoming the head of their husband's household. Parents of daughters have the burden of scraping together dowries large enough to attract suitable husbands. The bigger the dowry, the better the prospect, as few families will allow their sons to marry dowry-less wives.

Xeni helps her sisters flip the rug over, and the two younger girls resume the rhythmic drubbing. When the wheat is harvested in the fall, they will replace the crushed straw in their mattresses with the fresh new stalks after the grain and chaff have been removed. Panagiota watches as her *Mama* readies the oven for the family's afternoon meal. She places two bundles of grapevine trimmings in the domed, outdoor oven and sets them ablaze. The walls of the kiln-like oven will have time to absorb the heat while she prepares the fresh ingredients from their garden.

By mid morning, the rugs have been beaten and left in the sun to air out. *Mama* sends Panagiota to the pit where the fire ash is dumped to retrieve two fresh buckets of lye. Panagiota scoops it out carefully with a piece of flat wood from a spot farthest away from the recently dumped ashes. It takes many months for the black and gray ash to transform into the brilliantly white lye. To Panagiota, each scoop looks like the thick, creamy yogurt her *Mamá* makes from their goats' milk. Her mouth waters, and she feels the renewed pangs of hunger as she makes her way back to the house with the heavy buckets thumping against her legs.

Her mother passes her, heading in the opposite direction, carrying a large copper pan with a tight-fitting lid that conceals its contents. She sets it down on the ledge in front of the oven, so she can push the white hot ash and glowing coals to the back before sliding the pan into the oven and sealing the opening with a heavy square of metal. She secures it in place with a large rock then steps back to fan the heat from her face. The food will cook slowly over the next several hours, tantalizing everyone with mouth-watering aromas and the promise of a warm meal.

Panagiota shakes off her thoughts of food to refocus on whitewashing the walls of their home. Dimetra brings water from the well to thin the caustic lye, so it brushes onto the cool stone walls more easily. When the inside and exterior of the house are done, they will freshen and whitewash the well, the cooking oven when it cools, and the small stone shower/outhouse. It's another one of Panagiota's favorite jobs. It makes everything look clean, fresh and orderly. And, the sooner they finish with the lye, the sooner their hands will heal.

They are nearly finished with the inside of their house when their *Mamá* calls out, "Panagiota! Dimetra! Put your brushes down and run to the mill to get your father. Our meal is ready! Xeni! Bring Tasia and help me cut some bread."

"I DON'T KNOW WHAT IT IS ABOUT FOOD YOUR MOTHER MAKES FOR YOU, ESPECIALLY WHEN IT'S SOMETHING THAT ANYONE CAN MAKE, ...BUT IT CARRIES A CERTAIN TASTE OF MEMORY."
— MITCH ALBOM

As soon as *Baba* arrives, the entire family clatters ravenously to the table. Panagiota immediately notices something different. There are *two* copper pots of food on the table *and* fresh baked bread! Her *Mama* brushes the wood ash from the copper lids before removing and holding them upturned under her ladle as she carefully fills everyone's plate with a steaming, saporous stew of potatoes, green beans, crushed tomatoes, garlic, onions, oregano and olive oil.

Fasolakia Yahknee! Panagiota confirms silently and excitedly to herself.

"What's in the other copper pot, *Mama?*" Dimetra and Panagiota ask in unison; too hungry and curious to acknowledge the coincidence.

"*Manestra,* (handmade, rice-shaped pasta cooked in chicken broth with tomato and olive oil)," *Mama* replies, "one of your favorites!"

Panagiota and Tasia smile and exchange a look of excitement then bewilderment, wondering what special occasion could possibly call for such a feast. Their eyes follow their *Mama* as she looks to their father in silent supplication...then to Xeni who appears to gloat, already well aware of the message Baba begins clearing his throat to deliver.

"I am taking Xeni to America to find a husband," he announces.

Clunk! Panagiota intuitively hears the second *papoutsi* fall into place. Complete silence follows, the feast momentarily forgotten, before a trumpet of questions erupts.

"What?" Exclaims Panagiota.

"When?" Demands Demitri.

"How long will you be gone?" Panagiota asks.

"Why can't she find a husband here in Greece?" Whines Tasia.

A familiar story flashes to the forefront of Panagiota's mind: *"Panagiota, you were the present Baba brought back to me from America after being gone so long."* Five years...the difference in age between Xeni and her. *Oh no!* She thinks, as the possibility of her father and sister's extended absence begins to register. She sees tears start to glisten in her mother's eyes, and it causes Panagiota's eyes to sting and well-up in response. She sees similar tears wobble on the lower lids of her sisters too, as if her family is a single, living organism.

"We will leave in the Fall at the end of the harvest," *Baba* states firmly, trying to restore the family's equilibrium, "…as soon as our paperwork is ready. When I have saved enough money, I will send for the rest of you to join us. While we are away, I want you girls to help your uncles in the fields and your mother in the house… especially when your new baby brother or sister arrives."

"*WHAT?*" All eyes swivel to their mother's slightly rounded belly.

C H A P T E R 2

PREPARING FOR THE TRIP
1918

The ensuing months are a blur of familiar and foreign activities. Two of the family's four donkeys are sold…preserving the strongest 2 for the mill and travel. In their place appear a new pair of shoes, a bolt of fabric and a gabardine coat. Xeni is fitted for a dress that her mother cuts and sews from the brown fabric with white circles, something Panagiota has never seen before. *Baba* takes one of the remaining donkeys down the mountain on several trips to meet with immigration authorities and purchase tickets for their voyage. Somewhere amid the upheaval, the girls learn that their new baby brother or sister will be born in February, but *Baba* and Xeni will not be able to greet the seventh Athanasouli child. *Mama* and *Baba* pray every day that the baby will be a boy to take over the mill, the house, the land…and bring a wife and her dowry to the family, but it will be many years before he is old enough for that. All the while, Panagiota, Dimetra and Tasia secretly hope for another sister.

Preparations for the trip consume every resource and what little free time the family has. There is no time for schooling, but Panagiota continues to work on her letters over the next few months to surprise her *Baba*. When planting season arrives, the family works the soil and sows seeds preserved from the previous year's crops. The seedlings struggle against the rocky soil and arid conditions, yielding only the most truculent crops. They carefully tend the garden, fruit trees and grapevines, drying the grapes into raisins on sheets of fabric stretched on the ground. Sometimes Mother Nature is cruel. If it rains on the golden clusters of grapes before they are picked, or while they are drying, they become spotted and cannot be sold for the best price at market, or worse, rotted. The family has to move quickly to cover the fruit still on the vines with fabric, or bundle and drag the sheets heaped with partially-dried raisins into their already cramped house until the rain stops.

After the hot, dry summers, everyone relishes the cooler Fall weather that makes the backbreaking harvest bearable. The ripening fruits, nuts, olives and wheat impose a furious work ethic. The livelihood of the family, and now *Baba* and Xeni's trip, depends upon the success of the harvest. Apricots, cherries and dates are eaten, bartered, dried or preserved. Xeni, Panagiota and Demitra climb the olive trees to shake the ripening fruit off the branches onto awaiting sheets of fabric below. By the time the Kalamata olives are pressed or brined, the almonds and walnuts are ready for gathering. They are more easily stored, and their protein and fat will keep the family's hunger at bay during the cold winter months.

The end of the harvest is usually cause for celebration, but this year the misery of the season is extended by the dread of *Baba* and Xeni's impending departure. The taxing, physical demands distract everyone from the turmoil of emotions that swirl tighter and tighter inside them as the deadline approaches. The sisters work lethargically as if delaying the harvest will somehow forestall their family's disintegration. As winter approaches, the grape vines are cut harshly back; the trimmings, once again, bound into stackable bundles. Seeds for next year's vegetable garden are carefully dried and stowed. And of course, the year 'round care of the donkeys, lambs, goats and chickens continues.

A Change Of Plans - 1920

Issues with Xeni's travel papers develop, and their ominous Fall departure date comes and goes. Panagiota decides to buoy her father's sinking spirits by showing him the fruits of her secreted penmanship. She sits down next to him and writes out her name, first in Greek...*Παναγιώτα Αθανασούλης*... then in Roman lettering ... *Panagiota Athanasouli*

"When did you learn to do this, Panagiota?" Her *Baba* asks in astonishment.

Panagiota hears pride in his voice, and her face flushes with heat. But his pride is contradicted by a smudge of sorrow that also crosses his brow.

Oh, no! Did I do something wrong? She wonders.

At nine years of age, Panagiota doesn't understand how her proudest accomplishment, being the first of five daughters to write her own name in Greek and Roman letters, will dramatically alter the course of her life. Her exciting feat is like the toppling of a tree that unintentionally topples another tree…and another tree…and another. Her *twenty simple letters, perfectly formed*, somehow ignite considerable chaos in her household. There are heated exchanges between her parents and whispered conversations with her oldest sister that result in anger, tears and Xeni's palpable contempt toward Panagiota. These are not at all the reactions Panagiota envisioned.

The next week, Panagiota's father takes her by donkey to a larger village where the two stand very still, first side-by-side and then individually, in front of a black box balanced on three tall sticks. The owner of the box steps behind it and curiously hides under a dark blanket. A prudent move she understands a few seconds later when a bright explosion of light temporarily blinds her. Father and daughter then stay overnight in the same village with a maternal cousin before returning to the place with the black box. There, the man, no longer under the blanket, hands her *Baba a* flat package. Her father opens it and bends down to show Panagiota its contents. She is startled by the perfect, miniature images of *Baba* and herself. It is the first photograph she has ever seen, but she gets only a fleeting glimpse before her *Baba* carefully slips it back into its stiff protective sleeve. The two travel farther up the mountain on their donkeys to her *Mama's* childhood village for a two-day surprise visit with Panagiota's *YiaYia* (grandmother) and *Papou* (grandfather). Panagiota feels special being the center of everyone's attention and savors the rare opportunity as they travel back down the mountain to their own small village of Lafka. Several days later, on a cold December morning, she awakens to an empty bed and a subdued household. *Theo* (uncle) Kosta, her mother's brother, and Panagiota's sister Xeni are waiting outside by a wagon that is already hitched to the donkeys. Panagiota's mother tenderly dresses her in the brown and white dotted dress, the one sewn for Xeni. She stuffs the toes of Xeni's over-large pair of shoes with tufts of wool to make them fit Panagiota's smaller feet and completes her daughter's outfit with the fall-weight, gabardine coat.

"*Theo* (uncle) Kosta and Xeni are going to take you and *Baba* on a trip," her *Mama* finally offers with tears glistening in her eyes.

Panagiota is lifted up into the wooden wagon next to Xeni and handed a knapsack of food as her *Baba* climbs up, taking the reins from his brother. The four wave goodbye and set off down the mountain to the village of *Kiato* where Panagiota learns that a "train" to Athens awaits them. It is early winter and pleasantly cool. *Baba, Theo* Kosta, Xeni and Panagiota bump along the rocky switchbacks, winding their way past familiar sites…fallow vineyards and grazing pastures and the communal watering hole. They arrive at a small wooden platform next to two parallel and seemingly endless bands of metal on the outskirts of Kiato.

"This must be the place where we will find the "train," Panagiota surmises.

Xeni spreads a blanket nearby in the crisp sunshine and unpacks their lunch. There is an unconventional rhythm to the conversation as they eat. Then out of nowhere, the shrill scream of a whistle breaks the awkwardness and so startles Xeni that she begins to cry. Xeni looks at her little sister who notices her older sister's eyes growing slightly unfocused before Xeni collapses to the ground in a faint.

A flutter of activity ensues. *Theo* Kosta tends to Xeni while *Baba* quickly gathers up Panagiota and their belongings and bounds toward the wooden platform. Once there, he picks up a tall stick with a square of white cloth tied to the end and begins waving it wildly above his head. In the distance, at the base of an approaching plume of gray smoke, Panagiota sees a dark mass emerge and grow larger and longer against the horizon, like a large snake hissing black smoke. She looks for cues on how to interpret this unknown. She glances first at Xeni who is still lying on the ground…to *Theo* Kosta who is patting her cheek and speaking urgently to her…back to her *Baba* who appears to be excited…even happy about the serpent's approach. Such conflicting information! She shields herself behind her *Baba* and holds tightly onto his leg as the hulking monstrosity slithers to a stop and sweeps both of them into its belly.

New Experiences

There are people inside sitting in orderly rows! They appear relaxed and calm. There are clear glass windows, leather-covered seats with numbers stamped on small metal plates, bundled packages stuffed on the open shelves above the passengers' heads, and a jumble of scents: burning coal, food, spices, tobacco, sweat, wood, paint and metal. New physical sensations too as the train whisks Panagiota and her *Baba* at speeds faster than she has ever traveled through territory and sights that grow increasingly foreign. It is exhilarating and confusing! She sees the countryside give way to a blur of paved roads, large buildings and people dressed in clothes much different from what she is used to seeing in her village.

Some time later, the train stops and disgorges its occupants. Her *Baba* informs her they have arrived in *Athens*, the pride of every Greek. The birthplace of the greatest philosophers, leaders warriors and mythological Gods and Goddesses. Panagiota has learned about many of them in school. In her naivety, she imagines the possibility of glimpsing Zeus, Athena or Mercury and remains on high alert, eagerly scanning the masses. She and her father stay with distant relatives on the outskirts of *Athens* for two weeks while their travel papers are finalized. Then a less foreign contraption, a horse-drawn buggy, collects them for a short trip to Piraeus, the port city southwest of *Athens*. The driver eventually reins the horses to a stop in front of a boat...no, *a ship* her father tells her...so looming, it looks like an entire village afloat on the water. Panagiota tries to sound out the white painted letters that tower over her on the massive black and red hull that appear to shout the ship's pedigree. She is helped along moments later when she overhears a conversation and learns the ship is named the *King Alexander*[2], a 410' long ocean-going vessel

---

2 "UK | Scotland | Picture of 'Titanic iceberg' unveiled". BBC News. 28 July 2002. Retrieved 28 February, 2023. Interesting fact: "Nine years earlier, on 20 April, 1912, the S.S. Bremen (later renamed the King Alexander), while sailing from Bremen to New York City, passed through the somber debris field of the

with quadruple-expansion steam engines, twin screw propellers and a serviceable speed of 15.5 knots, but these words mean little to a nine-year-old girl.

"This is our ship, Panagiota", her *Baba* exclaims excitedly. "It will take us to America!"

"*America?*" Panagiota asks, confused.

Before she can begin to process this new information, her father directs her to a small row boat just big enough for three passengers and an oarsman. The man rows them through rough waters to the ship where they bob insignificantly, up and down, beside the ship's looming hull before being instructed to climb a 25 foot vertical rope ladder that leads to an opening on the side of the ship. The rope is fat and prickly against Panagiota's small hands.

Her father follows closely behind, encouraging her, "That's it, Panagiota! Keep going! Don't look down!"

She moves in a halting manner with wobbly knees and a trembling grip, shaken by so many overwhelming sensations. At the top, she is plucked off of the rope and whisked into the ship by two uniformed sailors. It is the second monstrosity that has swallowed her up.

How long will we be on this ship? She wonders. *How far away is this place called America...an hour's boat ride? A day's boat ride?*

She sifts for clues from the myriad stories about *Baba's* first trip to America to no avail. They have no luggage; nothing but the clothes on their backs, so it can't be far, she reasons. But her ruminations are cut short as she is enveloped in the crush of fellow passengers, surging farther into the ship. She starts to lose her bearings amid the towering bodies that smell of wool, fish and perspiration, but her *Baba* pulls her close. She clings tightly to his hand. Her panic is heightened when she realizes that the men and women passengers are being separated!

RMS Titanic. Passengers and crew reported seeing hundreds of bodies floating in the water as well as many deck chairs and pieces of wood. Since there was already a ship specially chartered by White Star line to retrieve any bodies, the S.S. Bremen did not stop to recover any. 316 bodies were later recovered with 190 returned to port, 113 buried at sea and 13 unaccounted for."

"Men to the left! Women to the right!" Barks the intimidating Greek ticket steward. "NO EXCEPTIONS!"

Panagiota grabs onto her father and screams, *"BABA!* DON'T LEAVE ME, *BABA!".*

Her father scoops her up and talks urgently to the steward. She buries her face in his neck to hide her fear. His scent reassures her, and she thinks of how her little sister Tasia cuddled into her neck not so long ago. It makes Panagiota's eyes sting and her heart clench. They begin moving again to the left...*together!* She is safe! He carries her deep into the depths of the ship, down strange metal stairs and through long, skinny hallways to a very large room with rows and rows of metal beds stacked three high and a long table lined with chairs on both sides. Her father takes the lowest bunk. Panagiota is placed in the middle bed, and their new acquaintance from their row boat climbs into the top bunk. That night Panagiota cries silently... secretly...in her lumpy bed...for her *Mama*...for Tasia...for their newly cleaned and whitewashed home, silently repeating her supplications over and over again before spiraling into an exhausted sleep.

Steaming To America
(December 16, 1920)

Moments later, or so it seems, Panagiota is gently awakened by her *Baba* with the promise of food. Is it morning? Night? It is impossible to tell because there are no windows below the water line in the steerage. There are, however, strange bits of fire glowing inside glass bottles that magically light the narrow hallways. *Baba* escorts her to the dining table crowded with fellow passengers where they are served weak tea, hard bread and bowls of pasta covered with a thin tomato sauce. She eats because she is ravenous, but it is not as good as her *Mama's manestra*. The thought causes her throat to constrict around a dry crust of bread. Over the next 20 days, she and her *Baba* are served the same meal. It is enough time for nine-year-old Panagiota to squeeze her sadness and homesickness into a place deep inside her heart that she is careful to explore only when she is alone and no one can witness her fear or salty tears.

During the day, she quietly observes the astounding new things that surround her. There are strange toilets and smooth, white sinks with endless streams of water that come out of shiny metal spouts at the turn of a lever. She and her *Baba* try to keep their faces and hands clean, but there are no facilities and little privacy to wash their bodies and no clean clothes to change into even if they could. There are no candles or lanterns, just the strange lights that turn "on" and "off" at the press of a button on the wall. She is able to go outside, but it is bitterly cold. Her lightweight gabardine coat and black leggings do little to shunt the freezing temperatures, so she stays below deck in the warmth of their berth most of the time.

During the journey, she learns that the ship, part of the *White Star Line*, will take her and her *Baba* to a place called *New York City* in America. From there, *Baba* tells her they will go to a village called *Shelby, Ohio,* where her father's brother owns a cafe where they will live, and *Baba* will work. Panagiota envisions a whitewashed stone house with wooden shutters similar to her own and wonders how they will make room for two more people...and two more mouths to feed.

Three weeks later, on January 5th, there is a palpable energy among the passengers. *Baba* excitedly informs her that they will be arriving in New York City today. Without the burden of baggage, they move freely up and down the deck to catch their first glimpse of land since leaving Piraeus. Panagiota is overwhelmed by the sights as they enter the harbor. The land is flat, but the buildings are tall like mountains, bigger than any village she has ever seen! Their ship, which once overwhelmed her with its size, is now dwarfed into insignificance. During their voyage, Panagiota learned she could glean the most information when she receded into the background, quietly listening and observing. And so, as their ship steams into this strange new place, she stays very still and quiet at her *Baba's* side, soaking up tidbits of information.

The ship anchors just off a small island within sight of the glittering structures and an enormous green statue of a woman, holding a flaming torch. The ship's crew members shuttle 25 passengers at a time by rowboat to the island where they are herded into a building that is bigger than any Panagiota has ever entered, "*...For processing our paperwork,*" her *Baba* informs her.

It is warm inside! She sees magnificent, soaring ceilings with large arched windows that flood the interior with light. The floors are made of smooth speckled stone (*not dirt!*). Shiny white tiles cover the walls from floor to ceiling. She reaches out to touch them. They look wet and slippery, but they are dry to the touch! She and her father are herded like goats and sheep through a maze of roped-off lines with big signs that Panagiota cannot read. Their eyes are checked for signs of jaundice, their hair for lice and so on until their medical health is vigorously vetted. Fellow immigrants who fail even one of these tests are promptly returned to their ship for deportation back to their points of origin. The two travelers from Lafka may be filthy and tired, but they are healthy, so they move successfully to their final queue under an overhead sign that reads "O-H-I-O", the name of the place in which they intend to settle. Once they reach the front of the line, *Baba* is peppered with more questions by an official and an interpreter who speaks Greek!

"Papers, please."

Panagiota watches as *Baba* hands the man their two small red leather booklets with gold embossed letters that hold their magical photos.

"What is your name?" The official asks.

"Athanasios Athanasoulis[3]," Her *Baba* replies.

"What country are you from?"

"Greece."

"What village did you come from?"

"Lafka."

"How old are you?"

"Forty."

"Who is this little girl with you?"

"My daughter."

"Her name?"

"Panagiota Athanasouli."

"Age?"

"Nine."

"What is the name of your sponsor here in the United States?"

---

3 Athanasoulis and Athanasouli are used in the masculine and feminine forms respectively in accordance with the Greek language.

"Giorgios Athan."

"Relation?"

"He is my brother."

"Your name is Athanasoulis not Athan…"

"Yes. My brother is also an Athanasoulis, but he shortened his name when he came to America."

"Is he aware of your arrival?"

"Yes."

"Do you have proof?"

Her father produces a letter from Georgios which the official quickly scans and tucks into a folder with their other immigration papers.

"How long will you be living in the U.S.?"

"Two to four years."

"Do you have a job?"

"Yes, I will be working in my brother's restaurant."

"I'll need the name and address of the restaurant."

Panagiota's father hands the official a slip of paper that reads: The Crystal Restaurant, 214 W. Main Street, Shelby, Ohio. She watches as it also disappears into the official's green folder.

"Where will you be living and with whom?" The official probes.

"We will be living above the cafe in Shelby, Ohio," says her father, "with my brother Giorgio Athan…at the same address."

"Will your daughter also be staying at this address?"

"Yes. She will be staying with me."

This last exchange interrupts the rhythm of the interrogation. The official rubs his forehead with his hand as he exhales audibly. Panagiota and her father intuitively understand that his latest response presents a problem, and he hurries to expound.

"My brother Giorgio is getting married," Thanasi quickly interjects, "and his bride Sophia will take care of my daughter."

The official informs him that they will contact his brother to confirm his story. If everything checks out, their paperwork will be returned, and the two will be free to travel to Shelby, Ohio…and Shelby, Ohio only.

"You will know "if" and "when" your paperwork is cleared when you hear your names called at the bottom of the staircase," states the official translator. "If you do not hear your names, it means you have not yet been cleared, and you must return for the following day's roll call."

Thanasi acknowledges his understanding, and he and Panagiota sign their names on an important looking document. The official reviews and stamps it with a series of letters and numbers in red ink.

My signature was accepted by the official! Panagiota thinks with satisfaction. But her bubble of pride bursts just as quickly as she finally realizes that *this* is why *she* is here and her sister Xeni is not; *P-a-n-a-g-i-o-t-a A-t-h-a-n-a-s-o-u-l-i-*… *twenty simple letters, perfectly formed…*

Oh! Xeni never learned to write her name.

She and her father are abruptly dismissed, and a third official escorts them up an enormous, curved flight of stairs to a small, sterile room with a wall mounted porcelain sink and six bunk beds with blue and white ticked mattresses stacked to the ceiling in economical columns. She and her father are each handed a pillow and a blanket. They make their beds, introduce themselves to their newest roommates and settle in for their first night in America.

The following morning, Thanasi wakes Panagiota at first light, and the two encamp on the steps of the beautifully curved, wrought iron staircase; high enough to look down on the endless stream of immigrants being processed below, but low enough to hear the roll call of names that are barked out sporadically throughout the day. Much to Panagiota's dismay, they skip lunch, so they won't miss hearing their names. She is tired and hungry when the light streaming through the windows starts to fade, and the official shouts the final list of names for the day. "Athanasoulis" is not one of them. They will have to come back the following morning. It is dusk, and the glass ceiling lights, larger than the ones on the King Alexander ship, magically illuminate the entire building while masses of immigrants from all over the world are served a meal in a place called the *commissary*. The same lights just as magically blink off when she and her father return to their bunks exhausted, still unwashed, but at least satiated.

The next day, as they wait to hear their names again, Panagiota observes an unsettling sight: Men with skin the color of coffee, pushing brooms, collecting trash and polishing the windows and tiles. They pause now and then to spit a dark liquid into shiny brass containers tucked in the corners of the room. Panagiota has never seen a person with black skin before.

"Why is their skin so black, *Baba*?" She whispers with urgency. "And why are they spitting *BLOOD* into the pots on the floor?" The strangeness of the men frightens her, and she wonders if they are dying.

Four days later, in the main processing room, an authoritative voice calls out, "ATHANASIOS AND PANAGIOTA ATHANASOULIS...SHELBY OHIO! (Pause) ATHANASIOS AND PANAGIOTA ATHANASOULIS...SHELBY OHIO!"

"WE ARE HERE!" Thanasi shouts as he grabs Panagiota's hand. The two weave their way excitedly down the staircase. At the bottom, the official directs their progress by extending his arm, motioning to his left without interrupting his shouted monologue of names. At the next station, their paperwork is returned to them along with two train tickets to Shelby, Ohio, departing at 7:00 p.m. *Just two hours from now!* A small boat is arranged to shuttle them from Ellis Island to a train station on the mainland. This time it is less scary to Panagiota. She knows what to expect as they take their appointed seats on the train.

The man and woman sitting in front of them are beautifully dressed. They smell of perfume and cologne, and the woman has a small white box tied with a brown satin ribbon. A short time later, the woman turns to Panagiota, opens the box and offers her a sample of its contents. It is her first taste of chocolate and it is delicious! Everything in America is new, exciting...and overwhelming. Panagiota wants to stay awake to absorb it all, but it is dark again, and before she can stop herself, she slides into a heavy sleep.

SHELBY, OHIO
1921

The slowing of the train and the shifting of her father awakens her. "Time to get off the train, Panagiota," he says in tired, hushed tones. "We are in Shelby."

It is after midnight. The attendant in the train station points them in the direction of a street car with lights hanging on all four corners that are swaying violently in the January wind. Thanasi gives the driver the slip of paper with the name and the address of his brother's restaurant written on it and augments his rusty English with a brief round of charades. A short time later, the street car stops at the corner of West Main and Broadway where the driver gestures first to his last two passengers and then to the east, saying, *Crystal Restaurant.* He repeats himself, pointing first to an imaginary paper in his palm, to Thanasi and Panagiota…*"Crystal Restaurant"*…then out the streetcar door and to the East.

She and her father step down onto a cobblestone street and into a bitterly cold January night. It's more windy and biting than the winters in Greece and neither are dressed appropriately. They venture blindly down the street, looking for the cafe. There are lights in a window up ahead, and Panagiota dares to hope it is her uncle's restaurant. As they approach, the black and gold letters on the glass door of The Crystal Restaurant swing out toward them, disgorging two late night patrons. Thanasi deftly shelters his daughter in a nearby doorway and tells her to wait while he approaches the two men. She watches her father's now familiar game of charades begin anew...

"Thanasi Athanasoulis...Athan...Georgios' brother," he explains. "From Greece", he adds, patting both of his hands against his chest? "Georgios Athan?" He asks, pointing to the restaurant sign. "Crystal Restaurant?"

"Thanasi? George's brother?" Man #1 asks Thanasi to be certain. "From Greece?"

"Yes! Yes!" Thanasi says excitedly.

"It's George's brother...from Greece!" Man #1 says knowingly to man #2 out of the corner of his mouth without taking his eyes off their new acquaintance. "HE'S HERE!"

Panagiota watches from her hiding place as the two men shake her father's hand and slap him on the back. They reverse direction and all but carry him into the restaurant, shouting, "HE'S HERE! GEORGE'S BROTHER IS HERE FROM GREECE!" She watches as the gold and black letters on the door swing shut behind them, and she is left alone in the shadow of her unfamiliar doorway, far away from her home, shivering uncontrollably.

~ ~ ~

"At nine years-of-age, I couldn't grasp the magnitude of our journey," recalls Panagiota decades later. "At nine years of age, I couldn't anticipate the ways in which leaving my family would impact each and every moment of the rest of my life. If my *Baba* had told me I would never again see my *Mama*, my sisters, my home, or my village, would I have gone? Would I have had a choice?

No. I know now that my fate was sealed the moment I proudly wrote my name... *Panagiota Athanasouli...Twenty simple letters, perfectly formed* that would alter my life forever."

~ ~ ~

Before long, the hands of her transformed father reach out to Panagiota, extracting her from her hiding place. Her buoyant, smiling *Baba* pulls her into his arms with a crushing hug and a shower of kisses as he bounces her right into the warmth and jubilation of the cafe. She is proudly introduced and fussed over by Man #1, Man #2, cafe employees and two Greek men Pete and Mike who were in the process of closing the restaurant for the night. But all of these activities are thrown into reverse, as the men fire the stove back up to feed their new guests with corpulent platters of Greek food that speak to Panagiota of home and family…and safety.

As they eat, Thanasi is informed that his brother is gone.

Oh, No! Thinks Panagiota as she looks to her father for context.

The men tell Thanasi that his brother left earlier in the day for Cleveland, Ohio, to stay overnight with relatives before heading to New York City in the morning to pick them up.

"He had the wrong date," Pete, one of the Greek-speaking cooks, tells Thanasi. "We'll get word to him, and he'll be back late tomorrow. You're all he has been able to talk about! He is going to be so happy to see both of you!"

Despite the late hour, the weary travelers remove their grimy clothes to bathe for the first time in almost a month. Their clothes are boiled and laundered to kill any lice. *Baba* cleans up first then makes sure his daughter is scrubbed from head to toe in hot water with a strong but fragrant soap. It is the first and only time her father gives her a bath. The soap burns and reddens her skin much like the lye back home, but strangely, Panagiota welcomes it. After so long, her hair and skin are squeaky clean and fragrant. It feels heavenly! She is given an oversized night shirt and told they will have a new set of clothes for her in the morning. There are several rooms for rent on the two floors above her uncle's restaurant and a communal bathroom at the end of each hall. But tonight, she is grateful to hunker down next to her father, knowing their journey is over, that they are clean and safe and will soon be among family once again when Theo Georgios returns.

A New Day

Panagiota awakes in a panic from the oblivion of a cavernous sleep. It's the middle of the night and her father is gone! Her need to find him wins out over the terrifying creatures she conjures up in her imagination. She gathers her courage and darts from her room, feeling her way along the dark, unfamiliar hallways and down the creaky stairs to the restaurant.

"Please let him be in the cafe! Please let him be in the cafe!" She whispers to herself to shut out the less desirable scenarios that threaten to bubble up from her psyche. She follows the aroma of food, the sound of activity and the clatter of dishes that lead her right into the kitchen.

PSYCHE
WAS A BEAUTIFUL PRINCESS WHO FELL IN LOVE WITH EROS (CUPID), GOD OF LOVE, AND WENT THROUGH TERRIBLE TRIALS BEFORE BEING ALLOWED TO MARRY HIM. THE STORY IS OFTEN UNDERSTOOD TO BE ABOUT THE SOUL REDEEMING ITSELF THROUGH LOVE.

"Hello, little doll," says Pete as he spies Panagiota peeking around the doorframe of the kitchen. "You slept like the dead! But today is your lucky day! Your Theo Georgios is back, and you're just in time for dinner!"

Dinner? Didn't we just eat dinner? She asks herself. His words trigger the growling in her stomach as her mind whirls to bring order to her confusion. As if on cue, she hears her father's laughter, coming from the front of the cafe, and she bolts toward the only person anchoring her in this strange new place. *"BABA!"* She screams as she runs towards him at top speed. But her trajectory is interrupted as she is scooped into the arms of a man who looks like her father, but is not. He lifts her high in the air then hugs her.

"Panagiota! How's my little doll? I am your Theo Georgio! How are you?"

Panagiota is kissed and squeezed by this *stranger.* She squirms to break free, her arms outstretched toward her father who is beaming with pride, sitting at a table full of men; some of whom are familiar to her from the night of their arrival. Theo Georgio calls out jubilantly over his shoulder to the kitchen staff as he hands Panagiota gently over to his brother, "Panagiota is awake! Bring out the food! We can finally celebrate!"

Panagiota is presented with a clean set of clothes to replace her over-large nightshirt. She is taken to the cafe's bathroom by a kindly, older waitress who helps her wriggle into a soft white undershirt, black, opaque stockings and a brown, knee-length, long-sleeved dress with buttons up the back. Everything fits with a little room for growth. Panagiota returns to her *Baba* a few moments later, unable to hide her pride in her fresh new appearance and sits down at a table laden with Greek food. It is a celebration with boisterous conversation and laughter. For Theo Georgios, it marks the arrival of family and trustworthy help…for Thanasi and Panagiota, the end of an arduous journey with the promise of a prosperous new life in America. As the platters are cleared, a satiated Panagiota pops a fourth and final *Dolmathaki*[4] in her mouth. The heaviness she has carried in her shoulders finally lifts, and it occurs to her that it is also the happiest and most relaxed she has seen her father in a very long time.

"IF YOU REALLY WANT TO MAKE A FRIEND, GO TO SOMEONE'S HOUSE AND EAT WITH HIM… THE PEOPLE WHO GIVE YOU THEIR FOOD GIVE YOU THEIR HEART."
–CESAR CHAVEZ

A New Life

The following morning, Panagiota is introduced to a strange new breakfast, *American Corn Flakes*. They are good. Crunchy. But the milk is *cold* and tastes different then the milk from her village.

"It's milk from a cow. Not a goat," explains her Theo Georgio knowingly with a chuckle in response to the questioning look on her face. Then further information, "..like a goat, but much bigger."

"Yes?" Panagiota questions with a bit uncertainly, "…a cow?"

Her uncle nods in the affirmative.

"It's good!" Panagiota replies between spoonfuls.

As the days and weeks go by, Panagiota and her father settle into their new home above the Crystal Restaurant. She hears stories about the first time her father and Theo Georgio came to

---

4 *Dolmathaki* are ground meat and rice wrapped in grape leaves, cooked and marinated in lemon, olive oil, dill and salt.

America, looking for work with their two younger brothers Kosta and Panagiotis. Thanasi and Georgio's shared history and struggles make for a comfortable reunion and partnership. Thanasi washes dishes during the week, and takes turns cooking on the weekends. Panagiota busies herself, wrapping silverware in white cloth napkins near the cafe's front window where the sun streams in. It affords her a view of the horses, buggies and people that go by. She particularly likes watching the millinery shop across the street where women enter, looking quite ordinary...and exit transformed, smiling with confidence, wearing or carrying new, crisply-styled hats.

The owners, a nice young couple, live in the apartment above the shop. The wife is pretty. She smiles a lot and has a kind face. They have no children of their own, but Panagiota sees the couple's young nieces and nephews visit from time to time...like today. And this seemingly innocuous event is enough to rip the lid off the box Panagiota has kept securely shut inside her. And it is there, in the window of the Crystal Restaurant with her unique vantage point on her strange and wonderful new world, that she begins to cry uncontrollably. She cries and cries to the point of hiccups and hysteria.

Modern day photo of Mrs. White's
millinery shop and second floor apartment.

"What's the matter, Panagiota?" Her father asks as he hurries toward her from the kitchen, drying his wet hands on his apron and squatting down in front of her. Panagiota looks into her father's eyes

and tries with all her might to push the lid back down on her sadness, but it's as if its contents, but not the box, has suddenly doubled in size. A familiar Greek myth pops into her consciousness about Zeus giving Pandora a beautiful chest with the instruction to never open it. But she does, and all the evils and miseries of the world fly out to afflict mankind.

PANDORA
THE FIRST MORTAL WOMAN CREATED BY THE GODS AT THE INSTRUCTION OF ZEUS, OPENED A BOX, RELEASING ALL THE EVILS OF HUMANITY, LEAVING ONLY HOPE INSIDE ONCE SHE CLOSED IT AGAIN.

Panagiota (Pauline) Athanasouli at 9 years old.

Panagiota's stomach drops as she realizes she is about to let her father down, much like Pandora let mankind down. She can see in her father's eyes that he desperately wants her to be strong. Feelings of failure and weakness glob onto Panagiota's already runaway snowball of emotions. Her father intermittently hugs her and rubs his hands up and down her arms, trying to comfort her, but it only helps the snowball pick up mass and speed.

"What's the matter, Panagiota? Why are you crying?" He asks her over and over, but she is crying so hard now she can't compose herself long enough to answer. Her sobs, like the repetitive shriek of a fire truck, draw the entire restaurant staff from the kitchen to investigate the unfolding calamity. Panagiota is surrounded by caring people who want nothing more than to help, and yet, she somehow feels completely and utterly alone.

"What is wrong with me?" She wonders between sobs, thankful no one can hear her thoughts. And then, to her horror, with what seems like the entire world looking on, she betrays her own confidences, blurting out the answer to her father's question.

"I want to go home! I want Mama!" She blubbers through fits and starts and streaming tears.

A stilted chaos ensues…questioning glances, hushed conversations, confusion, uncertainty…and then the crystallization of a masculine, well-meaning, but wholly misguided plan of action. With false bravado, her Theo Georgio carefully cajoles her outside and into the front seat of his Chevy, the one with the plastic window coverings with metal snaps and curtains, certain that a drive through the small metropolis of Shelby, Ohio, will lift Panagiota out of her emotional spiral.

CHAOS

IS THE ANCIENT MYTHOLOGICAL VOID STATE (OR AMORPHOUS GOD-LIKE ENERGY) PRECEDING THE CREATION OF THE UNIVERSE FROM WHICH THE FIRST DEITIES EMERGED: GAEA (THE EARTH), TARTARUS (THE UNDERWORLD), EROS (LOVE) AND LATER EREBUS (DARKNESS) AND NYX (NIGHT).

Her Theo Georgios drives her by the park, the school, through a covered bridge, by a church with pretty stained glass windows, a baseball diamond and fields filled with cows and horses. He drives her by the biggest, fanciest house in town, which also happens to be the local funeral home, followed by the movie theater, a playground with swings and slides and the stately post office. He drives and drives… as Panagiota cries uncontrollably.

Forty-five minutes later, the Chevy pulls to an abrupt stop in front of the Crystal Restaurant. Panagiota returns to her familiar windowsill still weeping. A frazzled Theo Georgio slams his hat onto the counter, shrugs his shoulders, and with upturned palms, blurts out to no one in particular, "WHAT DO WE DO NOW!?!" It seems there is nothing anyone can do.

Then the phone rings. It is Mrs. White, the nice lady from the milinery shop across the street, calling for Georgios Athan. "I see your young niece crying in the window," she says through the receiver. "Why don't you bring her over to my shop. I'll entertain her and cheer her up."

"But, she doesn't speak any English," Panagiota's still shaken uncle cautions as he runs his free hand through his already disheveled hair.

"That's okay," soothes Mrs. White. "We'll get along just fine."

Paper Dolls

Panagiota's name is quickly Americanized to Pauline as her Uncle walks her across the street and introduces her to Mrs. White. The two spend that afternoon, sitting on the floor of the White's apartment, looking at colorful printed sheets of paper dolls. Mrs. White teaches Pauline how to use scissors to cut out their fancy printed wardrobes and "tab" them onto the dolls' cardboard forms. And after each visit, she lets Pauline take her newly-cut paper dolls and their

carefully clipped wardrobes back to the Crystal Restaurant.

Her father and her much relieved Theo Georgio provide her with lidded cigar boxes in which to keep her treasured doll collection safe. And slowly the beauty and enjoyment they provide helps soften the ugliness of Pauline's homesickness. She names three of the paper dolls after her sisters, and together, she and her reassembled family conjure-up make-believe trips to Mrs. White's hat shop and all manner of errands that require frequent wardrobe changes.

At the start of their third week of play dates, instead of scissors, Mrs. White hands Panagiota a square piece of white fabric. She cuts out the shape of a bird from a remnant of the same cloth and shows Pauline how to backstitch it onto the larger fabric with contrasting blue thread. Panagiota now has the attention of a nurturing mother figure and two new hobbies to help fill her time at the cafe. They help form a protective bandaid over the hole in her heart that Pauline never knew her mother and sisters filled so perfectly.

Eager to forestall a future emotional debacle, Pauline's father enrolls her in the final few months of classes in the local public school. She enters the second half of third grade with children who are one year younger. Still, the language and cultural barriers make it difficult for her to assimilate. She doesn't know any of the rules in this strange new country. Coincidently, her new teacher is also Theo Georgio's American girlfriend. The two talk and flirt during Pauline's pick-up and drop-off times, something she doesn't imagine a *good Greek girl* would do. Yet Pauline grows to like her teacher who spends extra time helping her throughout the week. Pauline slowly learns to write the entire Roman alphabet and a few simple American words. But, she is still relieved at the end of each school day when she can return to the comfort of the cafe, and the rhythm and palliation of her paper dolls, her embroidery and everything soothingly Greek.

Sundays are especially enjoyable. The cafe is shuttered, and Pauline gets to spend the entire day with her father and Theo Georgios as they drive to the closest Greek church two hours away in Columbus, Ohio. It is a much fancier church than her family's simple chapel back in Lafka, Greece. Pauline studies how the Greek-Americans act and is in awe of the glittering, life-sized effigies of Jesus, Mary and the Saints that adorn the altar. They are painted in vibrant, flowing robes with halos and highlights of shimmering gold leaf. There is a soaring, domed ceiling, depicting heaven in the round with a spectacular crystal chandelier lighting the way to salvation. The priest wears a tall, cylindrical hat with a flat top called a *Kalimavkian* and a matching, floor-length robe beautifully embroidered with gold thread; so elegant in comparison to the little bird appliqué she recently learned to sew with Mrs. White. Pauline resolves to learn fancier stitches as soon as possible. She finds the ritual of the Greek church service with its analeptic order of events very soothing; the familiar smell of incense, the calming chanting of the priest, the stern sermons, and her favorite part... the freshly cut cubes of communion bread that the priest drops dismissively into her open palm as she genuflects and kisses his ruby ring. Beyond its symbolic relevance, the bread serves as an appetizer for the second half of Pauline's Sunday afternoon ritual, a delicious meal served at the home of fellow Greek-Americans Jim and Bill Kanellos (Americanized to Kanel).

The Kanel brothers' wives are excellent cooks, and today's meal is a mouth watering combination of *Pastichio* (a mixture of baked pasta, ground lamb, tomato, onions, and cinnamon topped with a creamy béchamel sauce), *Tomato Salata* (tomatoes and cucumbers dressed in olive oil, vinegar, oregano, salt and pepper), *Radikia* (dandelion greens cooked and drizzled with olive oil and lemon juice), *Feta* Cheese, *Kalamata* Olives and more crusty, warm bread. Mmmmh!

Pauline quietly savors the food as she gleans tidbits of information that float down to her ears from the adults' discussions. If she is quiet enough, they often say things they normally would not in her presence. This Sunday she learns about the final negotiations of an arranged marriage between one of the Kanel brothers' sisters, who is still in Greece, and Theo Georgios. Her uncle tentatively agrees to the union with the hard fought caveat that he gets to see her in person before making his final commitment. The discussion revives a memory of her father's conversation with the official at Ellis Island when they first arrived in America...

Official: "Is there a woman in the household to look after her?"

Baba: "My cousin Georgios is getting married, and his bride Sophia (Kanellos) will take care of my daughter."

A Wedding
(Shelby, Ohio 1921)

Over the next several Sunday dinners, a timeline for Sophia's arrival from Greece, her "inspection period" and a wedding date are argued back and forth with gusto and emotion before a final agreement is struck. The prospective joining of the two families is celebrated with a round of *ouzo* (a Greek, licorice-flavored liquor) and *baklava* (a dessert of paper-thin *Filo* dough brushed with butter, and layered with a mixture of chopped walnuts and cinnamon sugar, that's rolled, baked, cut and drizzled with honey) and of course strong, black coffee to keep Thanasi and Theo Georgios awake for the two-hour drive back home to Shelby. It's late when the trio return home, but not too late for Pauline to pull out her special cigar boxes and share the exciting news.

"A marriage has been arranged for Theo Georgios," she confides to her paper family. "Her name is Sophia Kanellos...

Kanel… and she is coming to America from a larger city in Greece, though not too far from our village."

"Oooh!" Exclaims paper doll Dimetra. "I hope she is pretty!"

"…and nice like Mrs. White," chimes in paper doll Tasia.

"If she isn't, Theo Georgios doesn't have to marry her," Pauline explains. "He gets to see her first before he decides."

"What happens if Theo Georgios looks at her and decides he doesn't want to marry her?" Asks paper doll Dimetri.

Pauline pauses as she considers the answer to her own question. "It's way past your bedtime," she tells her dolls as she tucks them into their boxes and slides them under her bed. But she imagines the answer must be something bad since the possibility has never been discussed at their Sunday dinners.

Thea Sophia

"She is here! Her name is Sophia, and she is from Tripoli, the third-largest city in Greece," Pauline tells her paper sisters. Then in hushed tones, "I really wanted to like her…but I don't."

She is pretty…at least pretty enough for Theo Georgios to marry, but there is something about her that reminds Pauline of her older sister Xeni. Sophia is nice to her when her Uncle Georgios or father are around, but she ignores Pauline completely, or worse, when they aren't. In many ways, they should be cut from the same Greek cloth, but the warp and weft of their characters seem to seep out of their pores differently. Sophia maintains an air of superiority and a compulsive need to be the center of attention. She has a strong need to be in control and is adept at manipulating people and events to that end.

Shortly after their simple wedding ceremony, Theo Georgios comes home with a beautifully wrapped present for his new wife. Sophia unwraps it and finds the dress she has been admiring in one of Shelby's finer shops. It is fancy like the paper dresses Pauline cuts out for her dolls. Sophia is over the moon until she notices the same dress on sale in the shop's window a few weeks later and demands that her new husband return the dress immediately. She can't have people thinking she can only afford dresses that are on sale!

Before long, Sophia also becomes dissatisfied with their rented living quarters above the Crystal Restaurant, even though it is nicer than the home she left behind in Greece. Nevertheless, Theo Georgios rents a bigger, two bedroom house a short walk from the cafe. Sophia revels in her improved status, but is overwhelmed with the additional housework, so Pauline is asked to help her on the weekends.

The two work side by side at first, but before long, Pauline is responsible for nearly all of the housework. When anyone comes to the house, Sophia quickly grabs a cleaning rag to hold in her hand before answering the door to keep up appearances. And for the neighbors' benefit, she periodically shakes out the dust from Pauline's used dust rags on the back porch. Pauline pretends not to notice. She enjoys the satisfaction of an honest day's work and contents herself knowing that while housework is tiring to one's body, Thea Sophia's attempts to project and maintain a false image must be exhausting to her soul.

Pauline (10), Theo Georgios, wife Sophia and Thanasi.

Theo Georgios and Thea Sophia's first child, a boy named Angelo, doesn't survive infancy. Their second child, a girl, arrives midway through the following school year. Pauline thinks about her mother back in Lafka, certain that she must have had her baby by now and wonders, *Do I have a new sister or a brother? Does she or he know about me? Will I ever see them again?* Then she silences her thoughts, putting a lid back on her stirred-up emotions. *I am here, now, and thinking of them will only make me sad. I will not embarrass myself with another bout of tears and homesickness.*

As Thea Sophia recovers from the birth, she relies on Pauline's daily help. At ten-years-of-age, Pauline walks from the Crystal Restaurant to her Theo and Thea's house before daylight and walks back to the cafe each night for a late dinner. In addition to housekeeping, Pauline is expected to cook the family meals and care for the baby. Xenia is tiny and cute. Sometimes Pauline stays overnight, to give the baby her bottle, so her Thea can rest. Her aunt places a rug on the floor near Xenia's crib for her niece and unpaid housemaid to sleep on. It is tiring work, but Pauline reasons that it will only be for a few more months. And she experiences a greater sense of freedom at night, a luxury she doesn't enjoy during the day under her Thea's watchful eye. For Pauline, baby Xenia is like a living paper doll that she can bathe, dress, snuggle, talk and sing to. The baby grows to love and depend on Pauline and helps lighten the sadness in her heart.

Thanasi, Pauline and Xenia

As fall approaches, Thanasi tells his daughter, "Panagiota, Thea Sophia and baby Xenia like you so much, they want you to keep coming to the house every day!"

There is no mention of returning to school. Pauline smiles, thinking about Xenia, but her smile quickly slips as reality sinks in.......*If I'm at their house every day, I won't have time for school.*

While her fourth grade classmates are learning to read and write, Pauline's homework will be full time housekeeping and nannying.

Pauline is accustomed to the demands of her aunt, but not the growing hostility directed toward her. There are no words of praise. Pauline's only compensation is her daily lunch and the *training* her aunt repeatedly tells her she is "…lucky to receive." In fact, the more work Sophia shifts to Pauline, the more difficult, demanding and ungrateful her aunt becomes. And it occurs to Pauline that Sophia resents her because she is one of the only people who sees behind her carefully constructed facade.

Sophia has needs that are difficult to anticipate and standards that are even harder to achieve. When Pauline is unable to measure up, her aunt berates her. Before long, Sophia's harsh, demeaning words are accompanied by dismissive shoves, but only when the two are alone. She is careful to maintain a different image when her husband is home, greeting him at the door, faux cleaning rag in hand, and fawning over him…and her niece…like a mother hen.

One frosty evening when Theo Georgios is working late at the cafe, Pauline finds herself alone with her aunt in the kitchen. Sophia is chopping onions as Pauline feeds Xenia an early dinner in her high chair. The baby playfully bats the spoon, splattering baby food on herself. As Pauline leans forward to clean her up, she feels a searing blow to her head punctuated by a string of harsh invectives. She recoils, turning shocked eyes to her attacker as her hand instinctively flies to her injury. Time slows down and it's as if she sees herself from the height and safety of the uppermost branches of a tree; the anger in her Thea's face and the glint of the knife, still in her hand with bits of chopped onion and strands of Pauline's hair clinging to the blade. A rivulet of blood courses down Pauline's scalp triggering her adrenalin, and all of a sudden, she is RUNNING!

From the safety of her tree, she watches her injured self lurch out of her chair and into the hallway. She witnesses herself grab her coat and use her hat, the one knitted by Mrs.White, to staunch the bleeding as her cut pulses and screams. She sees herself run out the front door, down the porch steps and onto the sidewalk leading to the Crystal Restaurant, swinging her free arm as hard as she can to stay ahead of her raging shock, burning tears and seething anger. She runs past the safety of the doorway where her father once hid her and yanks open the restaurant door with the black and gold letters on the glass. She runs straight to her Baba in the kitchen, removes her saturated hat, brandishing the bloody evidence, certain that it will finally expose her Thea, as she bares her soul to her father for the second time. "I WANT TO GO HOME! I WANT TO GO BACK TO *MAMA!*" She demands with uncharacteristic authority.

The emotional hooligans that nipped at her heels all the way from her aunt's house suddenly catch up to her and deliver a sucker punch as if to punctuate the finality of her father's devastating reply....

"You can't..."

OOOMF!

The Thread Is Cut

Pauline never finds out whether her father says anything to her uncle about Sophia or the gash on her scalp. She is not part of any discussions about it. She only knows that she is expected to go back to help her aunt the following day as if nothing happened. And during the game of silence that ensues, her mind starts to play tricks on her....

It wasn't so bad.

Maybe I imagined it. It's probably my fault. I should have been more careful.

But the blood encrusted ridge on her scalp acts as a touchstone of proof; her fingers, the jury repeatedly worrying and weighing the evidence and her Aunt's guilt. But the silence and the inaction of Thea Sophia, Theo Georgios and her own father become powerful and insidious foes that slowly disfigure the truth, turning it inside-out; playing mind games with her.

She didn't mean to do it.

I deserved it.

Secrets and the uncomfortable truths behind them are often altered and manipulated, shifting blame to innocent victims, because it is incomprehensible to others that such evil intentions exist. The injury to Pauline's scalp is painful, but it will heal. But the loss of trust in her aunt, her uncle…and most importantly her father…irrevocably changes her.

When she returns to her aunt's house the next day, Sophia acts as if nothing happened. Outwardly, Pauline perpetuates the charade, but inwardly, she vows to never be caught off guard again. It requires constant vigilance. She sees less and less of her father as her responsibilities at her uncle's house continue to grow. She has learned first hand that depending on anyone other than herself is fraught with hurt and disappointment. She becomes self reliant and self sufficient. She interacts with adults when necessary, but feels safest when she can retreat to an island of her own making. She walks to her uncle's house each morning and returns to the Crystal Restaurant each night to eat her dinner in the kitchen as her father cooks or washes dishes. He asks about her day, and she tells him superficial stories about baby Xenia. If he notices the welts or bruises, he never lets on. Their mutual silence makes it easier for both of them to pretend everything is fine…but it causes Pauline's emotional connection to her father to wither.

Her third September in America rolls around. Baby Xenia is now 15 months old and walking. Pauline should be starting the fifth grade, but she has too much housework to do. There is little time to mourn the loss of her education or her own childhood. She begins her chores in the back of the house, so she doesn't have to witness the neighborhood children walking to school. It's easier that way. Then, over a Sunday dinner, she overhears exhilarating news. Thea Sophia is now tired of the small, unsophisticated town of Shelby. She is expecting a second baby and wants to move to a bigger home in the larger, more exciting city of Newark, which is conveniently closer to her brothers. It means her aunt and uncle will be moving. Pauline can barely contain her excitement! *Stay still, Panagiota. Listen!* She silently entreats her 12-year-old self. *Pay attention to what the adults are talking about. This is important!*

Discussions center around Theo Georgios opening a new restaurant and moving his family to Newark shortly before the second baby's arrival. Pauline begins to contemplate a life free of her aunt's aggression…and maybe even the possibility of returning to school. She happily spends the next several months with the added burden of packing her aunt and uncle's entire household for the move. With each sealed box, she feels a weight lift from her shoulders. It will be hard to say goodbye to Theo Georgios and especially baby Xenia. It seems that everyone Pauline cares about is always being snatched away, but Newark is only a short drive from the Greek church in Columbus, Ohio. She will be able to see Xenia each week after Sunday services at their weekly dinners.

The next few weeks continue on as usual. Pauline is now adept at suppressing her longing for her *Mama*, her sisters, her village and the abrupt circumstances of her departure, but on a cool Spring day, she is unexpectedly catapulted back to the moment of laceration.

CHAPTER 4

AN UNEXPECTED CONVERSATION
1923

She and her father enjoy their usual morning fare in companionable silence at the breakfast counter of the Crystal Restaurant: Pauline crunches her way to the bottom of her corn flakes while her father eats thick slices of buttered toast, washing each bite down with a sip of strong, black coffee.

"You have been a big help to Thea Sophia, Panagiota," her father says, complimenting her. "So much so that she and Theo Georgio would like you to live with them when they move to Newark."

…You…

Pauline is so blindsided by the implications of this single word that the mechanisms in her brain lock up. She stops crunching and looks up at her father in wide-eyed silence, which he chooses to interpret as quiet acceptance. So he continues.

"She will be able to take better care of you than I can here. You'll have a nice new home. You can help them unpack, and you'll be an even bigger help when the new baby comes."

Move to Newark…With <u>them</u>?

And just like three years ago when her mother dressed her nine-year-old self in the polka dot dress intended for Xeni…and the day Pauline couldn't stop crying in the window of the Crystal Restaurant…and everyone's indifference to the bloody gash in her head…she knows what *she* wants doesn't really matter. Her fate is already determined. She decides to send out a single, wobbly probe.

"Will you be coming with me, *Baba*?" She asks as she moves the hovering spoon of cornflakes slowly and deliberately into her mouth.

"No," he says. "I will stay here in Shelby to run the cafe, but we will see each other every Sunday at Church."

Pauline focuses all her energy on remaining still and swallowing the corn flakes that have suddenly turned into a distasteful paste. "When do I have to leave?" She asks without taking her eyes off her bowl of cereal.

"We will load all the furniture on a truck this week, so we can drive to Newark and unload everything after we close the restaurant on Saturday."

Her father is telling her all this in a forced, up-beat tone as if it is some kind of good news…or grand adventure.

"Then we will all go to church together on Sunday, and have our nice Sunday meal. You'll go back to Theo Georgios' new house, and I'll return to Shelby after dinner…"

"*Without ME!*" Pauline wants to scream in defiance. And as her composure slips, the question she really wants to ask nearly overpowers her carefully tempered self control. She clamps down on it just in time to stop its forward progress, causing it to ricochet against every cell in her body…

"*Why don't you want me?*"

"…Don't worry, Panagiota, we will see eachother every Sunday," her father continues as if this fact magically fills in the sink hole that has just opened up beneath her.

He is her only remaining link to her family, her past, her identity. Maybe he really thinks he is doing what is best for her. Then suddenly, a panicked, half formed thought rockets across Pauline's brain. *When Mama and my sisters come to America, how will they know where to find me?* But her brain is too overloaded to process this or any other thoughts right now. That night, as she lies in bed, her mind tentatively explores her father's words like one might circle an injured and cornered animal.

Y-O-U a-r-e m-o-v-i-n-g t-o N-e-w-a-r-k.

She absorbs the message from afar at first. And when the threat seems emotionally manageable, she moves in to investigate more thoroughly. *Twenty simple letters perfectly formed* that once again altar the course of her future. In some ways it is a relief to know things…even unsavory things…with some certainty. It ends the speculation and hope.

I am moving to Newark …by myself. Pauline thinks, trying on her new reality. She slips her arm through the thought to assess the fit as if it is a new garment. It feels two sizes too small and restrictive. It's spurious style makes bold and unwanted statements about her… about her future. She will be living with Thea Sophia and Theo Georgio almost two hours drive from her father and the Crystal Restaurant. She will not be going back to school in Newark. Her education will never progress beyond a fourth grade level. She will have a place to live and food to eat in return for her services: cooking, cleaning and taking care of Xenia and the new baby. And if she is lucky, she will see her father on Sundays. She ties the sash of her new, ill-fitting garment tightly around that final thought. It is the only thread that tethers her to the life she once knew…and the person she once used to be.

THE FATES
THE THREE GODDESSES THOUGHT TO PRESIDE
OVER THE BIRTH AND LIVES OF HUMANS. EACH
PERSON'S DESTINY WAS THOUGHT OF AS A THREAD
THAT WAS SPUN, MEASURED AND CUT BY THE
THREE FATES: CLOTHO, LACHESIS AND ATROPOS.

A New Home…A New Life

Heavy cleaning is required to ready the new house in Newark for the family's arrival. There are four bedrooms, one for Theo and Thea, one for Xenia, one for the new baby when he or she arrives and one for Pauline. But while she is allowed to hang her few possessions in the extra bedroom's closet, she is not allowed to sleep in the bed.

"It's a room for guests, not a housekeeper!" Explains Sophia dismissively.

A pallet is moved into a corner of the baby's room where Pauline is allowed to sleep on the floor. Her new life eventually settles into a pattern much like before. Every Friday, Sophia insists that the large wooden staircase be waxed and buffed to a shine. Pauline learns to apply the paste wax and burnish it to a shine by hand with a dry cloth. It takes most of the day, and her knees crack and bleed until calluses eventually form. She works earnestly over the next few months to balance the family's daily needs while setting up the entire household. Thankfully, the burden of moving is nearly complete when the new baby arrives; a little girl named Esther. Pauline's workload doubles overnight especially when Esther develops Whooping Cough. She sits up and rocks the baby night after night on her own small pallet, fearful that Esther will choke or die from her fits and intense fever. Pauline's only point of reference for Esther's affliction is a vague recollection of her baby brother Spiro who died back in her home in Lafka before his first birthday…when Pauline was only five.

Esther is too little to be wracked by such violent coughing. It breaks Pauline's heart as she holds the baby upright and pats her back to help clear the phlegm and soothe her as best she can. Pauline tenses with each new honking attack, instinctively swiveling Esther toward the corner of the room to help muffle her loud *whoops,* so they don't wake Sophia. Sometimes she sits with the baby on the floor of the closet, so the linens and hanging clothes absorb the noise. And always, there is the fear that Thea Sophia will storm into the room in a fit of anger.

After the sleepless nights, Pauline catches herself falling asleep during the day when she sits down to give Esther her bottle.

"Lazy!"

"Ungrateful!"

"Trash!"

She hears her aunt's harsh words, but she is too exhausted to bristle from the verbal attacks any more. After two weeks of sleepless nights, Esther's fever finally breaks and her coughing subsides. Pauline missed three straight church services, staying home to help Esther recuperate, but this week, Esther is finally healthy enough to go to church. Pauline looks forward to Sundays most of all. She gets to see her *Baba,* and after a hard week of work, the family drive to the Greek Orthodox church in Columbus offers a respite from her household chores.

Every Sunday morning, after cooking and cleaning up after the family's breakfast, Pauline bathes Xenia and Esther and dresses them in their best Sunday clothes. Baby Esther usually sleeps during the half hour car ride, and if Pauline is lucky, through the church service as well. Her father gives her a big hug when he sees her. Oh, how she missed him!

"How are you, little doll?" He asks, kissing her on both cheeks then scrutinizing her at arm's length. "You look so tired."

"Esther hasn't slept much these past weeks," she explains, "but she is better now."

After the service, everyone heads to one of the Kanel brothers' houses for Sunday dinner. Pauline watches the children while Sophia, keeping up appearances, helps her brothers' two wives set the table and plate the food. Pauline enjoys the banter around the table as everyone eats the well prepared meal. There is always news as *Baba* and Theo Georgio update each other on the business of their respective cafes.

AFTER A GOOD DINNER ONE CAN FORGIVE
ANYBODY, EVEN ONE'S OWN RELATIVES.
— OSCAR WILDE

Nine years tick by with few additional surprises. Thanasi continues to run the Crystal Restaurant. The Natoma Cafe, Georgio's new restaurant in Newark, prospers, and he and Sophia welcome their third and final child, a son named Angelo (Angel), or Angie for short, the same name as the first born baby boy who died. Pauline continues her role as nanny, housekeeper and cook as she grows into a young woman of 19. She hones her sewing skills learned from the kindly Mrs. White to sew not only her own clothes but also those of Xenia, Esther and Angie. Her only contact with the outside world is limited to the Greek Church community and Theo and Thea's houseguests. But Pauline's relationship with her aunt remains vastly different than Sophia allows others to see. Pauline has no money, no formal education and no independent means of transportation. She is expected to complete demanding physical labor 'round the clock for an unpredictable and abusive taskmaster who manages to diminish Pauline's "inconsequential" value each day before she falls exhaustedly onto her pallet on the floor…no better than a dog. But her cherished memories of her family back in Greece still tumble softly through her thoughts on a daily basis, updated here and there with snippets of news on special events from both sides of the Atlantic. There are no telephones in Pauline's village. Letter writing, although possible, is difficult. Pauline knows her Greek letters, but the spelling of only a few Greek words. And her expanding list of American words have no meaning to her *Mama* or sisters. Yet word of mouth somehow trickles back and forth: the 1918 Spanish Influenza that takes the lives of a neighbor and her two children while the woman's husband is working in America, the birth of her sister Eleni Athanasouli in 1920, only a few months after Pauline left; a sister just like Tasia, Demitra and she had hoped! Then five and six years later, the heartbreaking news of Pauline's seven-year-old sister Olga's death (1925) and the loss of another sister, beautiful Eleni, one year later.

A Family Reunion

1928 marks the ninth anniversary of Pauline and her father's time in America and the happy news from Greece that a husband has been found for 22-year-old Xeni, Pauline's oldest sister. Living frugally in Shelby and saving his wages from the Crystal Restaurant, Thanasi builds a nest egg that translates to a comfortable income in Greek drachma. He sends a modest dowry for Xeni to marry Philipa Karamani who uses the money to open a small gas station in their village. Thanasi also writes to summon his wife Kostandia and remaining, not yet wed daughters Dimitra (15) and Tasia (11) to America, so their family can be reunited and eliminate the future need for more dowries. But Thanasi receives an unexpected reply from his wife. She wishes to be reunited with Thanasi and Pauline, but she is torn.

"I have three children buried here, and Xeni is soon to be married," she writes. "How can I leave them? Come home to us, Thanasi. You are needed *here* in Greece."

Kostandina, Dimitra and Tasia will not travel to America. Thanasi and Pauline will need to return to their home in Greece. For Pauline, the change of plans accomplishes the same, long-wished-for outcome. But before her father can book their tickets, his brother Georgios entreats him to consider another last-minute proposal.

"Sophia's heart is breaking," Georgios explains. "She has grown to love Pauline as if she were her own child. Please! Let her stay here with us in America. We will take good care of her, and when she is of age, we will find her a good Greek/American husband. Please! Just think about it, Thanasi. There is more opportunity here for her here than in the old country. You know this to be true. Kostandina will eventually change her mind, and you can bring your whole family back to join us here in America. Until then, let Sophia and me take care of her. Panagiota will be better off. Please!"

Twenty more letters… *L-e-t h-e-r s-t-a-y h-e-r-e w-i-t-h u-s.*

Thanasi visits his daughter in Newark to say a brief, but tearful goodbye…and then he is gone. Nineteen-year-old Pauline is now old enough to understand the logic of staying behind; the opportunity for a better life, one less ticket for passage back to Greece and the promise of an arranged marriage in America without the dowry required in Greece. But emotionally…she is once again ostracized from the very thing that she cherishes and has wished for more than anything else, her family. It is another devastating blow.

(L to R) Pauline (19), Thanasi and the inserted image of Pauline's older sister Dimetra (18) still back in Greece.

After the news, Pauline's life continues in a topsy-turvy fog. For once, Thea Sophia's unattainable expectations become welcome distractions; the daily physical demands and long hours, a safe shroud of numbness. *Work hard. Survive, Pauline.* She tells herself. She may have only completed school through the third grade, but she has the equivalent of a master's degree in being self sufficient and self contained. And yet, the undercurrent of longing for her family never leaves her. Months later, on October 29, 1929, the U.S. financial markets collapse, marking the start of the Great Depression and mirroring the free fall of Pauline's shattered dreams.

CHAPTER 5

ISOLATED IMMIGRANTS

Immigrants often experience a difficult existence. They are physically estranged from their families, and to varying degrees, rejected by the citizens of their new homeland. They carry the weight of their family's hopes for a better life, sacrificing their own individual needs. It explains why immigrants often seek out fellow countrymen in their new countries, not to exclude others, but to create a semblance of the families and comfort they left behind. But misunderstanding, resentment, perhaps even jealousy, sometimes simmer below the surface from family members left behind in the *old country*. As Pauline mourned the loss of her mother's love and sisters' company, one of her sisters naively resented Pauline's life and experiences in America. Many who remained behind in Greece suffered greatly too. None more than Thanasi's youngest brother Panagiotis and his family.

Flashback to Tragedy

After the Athanasouli brothers' very first trip to America, all but Georgios return to Greece. Thanasi rejoins his young wife Kostandia and their four-year-old Xeni and quickly builds Lafka's first flour mill with the proceeds saved from his work abroad. Kosta and Panagiotis return a few years later and fight in yet another Greco-Turkish War (1919 - 1922), before starting their own families:

three boys and four girls for Kosta and his wife Stiliani and five sons and six daughters for the youngest Panagiotis and his wife Angelike.

Panagiotis' sons, Ioannis, Athanasios, Dimitrios, Basilios and Konstantinos grow into strong young men just as the Italians and Germans invade and occupy Greece during World War II. The Axis Powers quickly blockade Greek ports and initiate a policy of large scale plundering. A great famine ensues. Mortality rates peak during the winter of 1941–42 and remain grim until the end of the occupation in 1944.

During the winter of 1942, as 27 year old Athanasios, the second oldest of Panagiotis' five sons, shepherds the family's small flock of sheep and goats on the hillsides of Lafka, he encounters a German soldier. The soldier commands young Athanasios to turn his flock over to him to help feed the German military. Athanasios refuses. A fight breaks out, resulting in the German soldier's death. Fearing retribution, Athanasios shepherds his flock safely thome then hides in the remote caves outside the village.

The German commander, upon learning of the soldier's death, immediately dispatches a contingent of soldiers to their home, demanding to know Athanasios' whereabouts. When the family refuses, or is unable to tell the German soldiers, the father Panagiotis and his four remaining sons are violently removed from the house, taken into the fields. Panagiotis is forced to watch as each of his sons is savagely beaten and shot execution style.

The German soldiers return a badly beaten and emotionally broken father to his village, along with the bodies of his four sons with the warning that if any of the family or villagers are caught trying to help Athanasios, or any of the Athanasoulis family, they will meet the same fate.

"The entire village was terrorized by the German's unspeakable act," recalls Kiki Biniari, Pauline's niece and the daughter of Pauline's younger sister Dimetra. "Athanasios was my mother's cousin. He

Panagiotis and his wife Stiliani and their only surviving son Athanasios, his wife and two of their six children

would come out of hiding from time to time during that bitter winter, knocking on our door, begging for food, clothes, blankets… anything, but our mother and father would not let us answer the door. They were afraid of what the Germans would do to us. I was five years old at the time. My sisters Konstantina and Athanasia were three and two. All we could do was huddle in the corner, holding tight to one another in silence with our hearts in our mouths and tears streaming down our faces until his knocking stopped." Kiki's eyes glisten with tears as she relives the seventy-five-year-old memory.

Athanasios survives and comes out of hiding two years later after the German occupation. He eventually marries and has four sons and two daughters, fulfilling his expected role as the family's only male heir.

During these desperate times, Greek men continued to stream into America in search of opportunities that no longer existed in their own country. They came, emboldened by stories of the American Dream and the promise of better jobs with wages that would help lift up their struggling families back in the *old country*. They worked hard and experienced both hardships and varying levels of success. Some returned to their homeland, but many remained in America and built new lives, like the Pazos family from a village not far from Lafka whose lives will eventually intertwine with those of the Athanasulis family.

The Pazos Family

Jimmy Pazos, his Uncle Nick, brothers Mike and Pete and a cousin also named Pete, immigrate to America and build two successful restaurants in Toledo, Ohio: The Pullman, located on the second floor of a building in the downtown theater district and The Club Cafe, a restaurant favored by executives in the business district. The more swanky Club Cafe features carved mahogany booths with deep green leather upholstery and is one of the first upscale restaurants in the city to feature electric lighting and a carpeted dining room. "Cousin Pete" mans the register while Jimmy manages the restaurant, pays bills and builds excellent credit among their vendors. His exuberant personality and sharp business mind allow him to greet patrons by name, tell jokes and relay patron's detailed dinner orders to the kitchen by memory. He is a natural in the restaurant business and develops a loyal clientele. Jimmy's Uncle Nick and "Brother Pete" work as cooks while Jimmy's brother Mike floats in and out of the business. But when the Great Depression hits, Jimmy and his financial partner Cousin Pete wisely decide to close the Pullman and focus their time and resources on the more stable business clientele of The Club Cafe.

Friends, Family and Ghosts

The Pazos men enjoy a close relationship. Jimmy and Cousin Pete, along with four other men from their same village, all immigrate to America under the sponsorship of one of their cousins, while Jimmy's brothers Mike and Pete slip into the country illegally. The nine men initially find work as dishwashers and shoe shine boys. To economize, they rent a single room with four twin beds and work alternating shifts. As the first four men climb out of their beds in the morning to start their day, the four men returning from their night shifts climb into them. They are fed by their sponsoring cousin's wife who economizes by gathering up even the smallest pieces of uneaten bread at the end of each meal to recycle for the following day. The ritual so irritates Jimmy Pazos that he vows to become successful enough to afford fresh bread at every meal.

As their finances improve, the men eventually move into individual rooms at a nearby hotel with a communal bathroom on each floor. The only drawback, especially for Brother Pete is the view. His second story window looks out over a local cemetery, and Brother Pete is deathly afraid of spirits or anything to do with the underworld. It doesn't take long for the men to plan a terrifying, yet good-natured prank on him. They set their midnight plan into motion over lunch by fanning Brother Pete's fear of ghosts.

"Ask Brother Pete how he likes his new view from his room," says Uncle Nick as he niggles his nephew across the dinner table.

"Yeah, Pete, Harry says you've seen ghosts!" Mike says, feigning false alarm.

"*Mist!*" Clarifies an agitated Brother Pete. "I told him I saw *mist* rising from the graves after sunset." He glances over his shoulder and lowers his voice before adding, "It's the spirits of the dead."

"You can call them *ghosts* if you want," Cousin Pete says dismissively.

Affronted by the snickers of his dinner companions, Brother Pete shouts, "Go ahead! Laugh all you want, but that's what I saw!" Brother Pete pushes away from the table in disgust and storms out of the restaurant to smoke a cigarette and calm his jangled nerves.

Nick, Mike, Jimmy and Cousin Pete hold their laughter until Brother Pete is out of ear shot then begin fine tuning the details of their plan. During the tail end of the restaurant's dinner hour, Jimmy and Nick slip quietly up to Brother Pete's room to tie ropes around the legs of his iron bed frame. They conceal the ropes under the rug, tucking them along the baseboards, behind the curtains, up and over the window sill and out the open second story window until they coil neatly behind some bushes on the ground. They unscrew the lightbulb from the ceiling fixture to further camouflage their handiwork, then calmly return to the kitchen to eat a late dinner and help their unsuspecting victim close up the cafe. As they work, Nick and Jimmy tell stories about the cemetery and its nearby funeral home.

"Why do you keep talking about the dead?!" A rattled Brother Pete admonishes them. "You're going to bring their spirits right to our doorstep! Don't talk about them!" He says with finality as he spits three times to dispel any gathering spirits.

"Pete's afraid of ghosts," chirps Nick as Jimmy brushes the broom handle across Brother Pete's shoulder blades from behind.

"*Whooooooo!* Mocks Jimmy with a ghostly effect.

"*We're right outside your bedroom window, Pete!*" Says Cousin Pete.

A visible shiver runs through Brother Pete as he bats the broom away. "Very funny!" He barks with false bravado. "You're all morons!" He says, untying his apron. "Finish closing-up yourselves!" He throws his apron on the counter and stalks out of the kitchen.

The four tricksters briefly hold it together before bursting into laughter. Their trap is well laid. Brother Pete has plenty of *dead spirits* on his mind.

The tormentors wait until 2:00 am, then spend the next half hour outside Brother Pete's second story bedroom window, gently pulling the ropes...and Brother Pete's now occupied bed... intermittently and inch-by-inch, toward the window, without waking him. Their final tug is a sharp, jarring one designed to bang Pete's metal bed frame against the iron radiator in front of his window. It has the desired effect. The three pranksters are richly rewarded by an audible *shriek* and the slamming of doors as Brother Pete heaves himself out of bed, down the stairs and out of the building! Doubled over with laughter Mike, Jimmy and Cousin Pete weave their way back into The Club Cafe like guffawing drunks. Nick shrewdly returns to Brother Pete's vacated room to replace the light bulb and remove any evidence of their antics...except for Pete's bed. It is left in its new location, six feet across the room by the window with a birdseye view of the cemetery.

It is mid-morning before Brother Pete returns to The Club Cafe carrying a small brown paper bag. Nick winks at Jimmy before straightening his face and asking innocently, "Have you been out this morning already, Pete? We thought you were still sleeping."

"The light in my room burned out last night," explains Brother Pete, avoiding eye contact. "I had to run to the hardware store to pick up a new bulb."

"Maybe your ghosts made the light go out," chides Cousin Pete, unable to help himself. Brother Pete blanches and turns abruptly away, but says nothing.

Raising The Stakes

"*Nothing! That's it!*" Says a somewhat disappointed Jimmy as he finishes recounting the night's events to the rest of the restaurant staff later that day. "He didn't say a thing when he came back...not even about his bed!"

The conspirators decide to raise the stakes. During a friendly game of poker at Jimmy's house the following week, the men are merciless in their ribbing of Brother Pete, relentlessly pushing his fear of the spirit world to center stage.

"There's nothing to be ashamed of Pete," assuages Uncle Nick. "I know a lot of people who are scared of ghosts."

"I AM NOT AFRAID OF GHOSTS!" Seethes Brother Pete in an uncharacteristically strong outburst.

"PROVE IT!" The men counter in unison, throwing down the proverbial gauntlet.

Pete's eyebrows collapse briefly as he feels his manliness slip a notch before he crunches them defiantly together. "NAME IT!" He challenges.

"All you have to do…" Uncle Nick begins as the gears in his head begin quickly churning, "…is to go down to the funeral parlor…after midnight…and take one of the dead bodies out of its coffin…and carry it…"

"…OVER your shoulder!" Interjects Cousin Pete, pantomiming the movement.

"….over your shoulder…," Nick affirms, nodding his approval at Cousin Pete's brilliant contribution, "…to the restaurant and back. That's all," he says nonchalantly, dusting his palms against each other with an innocent shrug of his shoulders. "If you can do that, we'll all know, once and for all, that Panagiotis Pazos is NOT scared of ghosts…spirits…*mist*…or whatever you want to call them."

"Tonight…?" Asks Brother Pete in a wavering voice as he contemplates their dare. "I'LL DO IT!" He finally says after a momentary pause and with more certainty than the terrified look on his face would indicate.

Later that night, as the poker game progresses, Brother Pete drinks more wine and Ouzo than usual to fortify himself for his impending activity. It is now well after midnight. Jimmy pours a final double shot of Ouzo and pushes it towards his quaking brother. "You can do this, Pete," Jimmy encourages. "Just 30 minutes…a little walk…a little lifting…then no more teasing…ever. I promise! Cousin Pete, Nick, Mike…we'll all go with you. We'll stay with you the whole time."

During this brief coaching session, Uncle Nick does some *heavy lifting* of his own upstairs to make sure the night will be one that no one…especially Brother Pete…will forget. He strips a shirt, tie and a suit from a hanger and barges in on John, one of his co-workers.

"Put this on! Quick!" He says as he tosses a bundle of clothes at him. "I need you to run down to the mortuary, climb into one of the empty caskets and pretend you're dead."

"What?! Exclaims John.

"We bet Brother Pete he's too scared to carry a dead man over his shoulder to the restaurant and back," says Nick, hardly containing himself. You're going to be that dead man!"

"Tonight?" Balks the co-worker as he fumbles to put the suit on. "He's gonna recognize me!"

"No he won't," says Nick. "He's already had a few drinks. It's pitch black out, and (brother) Pete's scared half to death! Hurry up!"

With the *dead man* safely dispatched, Nick meets up with Jimmy, Mike and both Petes down in the cafe and pokes Brother Pete one last time to add fuel to the already blazing fire. "Listen, Pete," he says. "If you're too scared, you don't have to do this."

"I'M READY!" Pete says as he slams down the second empty shot glass, stands a bit unsteadily and stalks out into the night. Machismo, especially in front of one's male companions…makes for an amazing elixir! Nick, Mike, Cousin Pete and Jimmy race to catch up.

Brother Pete weaves boldly toward the funeral home. He heaves himself through an unlocked window and approaches an already open casket. His accomplices watch in disbelief as Pete takes a deep breath, hefts *John's* limp head and chest, then his entire body over his left shoulder without so much as a quiver. The four men help their staggering friend into the night and down the gravel road, accompanying him back to the house. Mike, Nick, Cousin Pete and Jimmy fall back two steps to pat their *dead* friend John's head. *Dead John* winks back conspiratorially, barely keeping a lid on his laughter.

"I can't believe he's doing it!" Mike whispers gleefully in Jimmy's ear.

Then, out of nowhere, there is the sound of something racing toward the men through the tall weeds, followed soon after by the barking of three territorial dogs. The ruckus shatters the night's calm and jumpstarts everyone's adrenaline. The men break into an all out sprint. Brother Pete falls behind under his ponderous load. Moments later, the dogs are nipping at his heels when the *corpse* on his shoulder grabs Pete's leg and yells, "LIFT ME UP HIGHER, PETE, BEFORE THEY TAKE A BITE OUT OF ME!"

There is an unhinged scream of terror, as Brother Pete throws his *not-so-dead-body* to the ground and takes off running into the night, yowling dogs in tow. The five accomplices fall down, laughing hysterically, congratulating themselves on pulling off one of the best pranks of all time.

Brother Pete doesn't return to the cafe for two full days, which provides adequate time for the three brothers, one cousin and *Dead John* to animatedly and repeatedly relay the story to restaurant staff and patrons. The men's relationship with Brother Pete survives despite the harsh initiation.

A Pazos/Athanasouli Wedding

In 1932, when Pauline is 21, Theo Georgio makes good on his promise to his brother. He approaches two single Greek-American men from the Greek community in Toledo as prospective husbands for his niece; Pete Pazos and his younger cousin James Pazos. Unbeknownst to Pauline, the two suitors are invited to dinner to assess their interest in her. Talks continue between the men after the meal at which time Cousin Pete decides he is not ready to settle down and backs out. But James agrees to the arranged marriage. A deal is struck, and Theo Georgios informs Pauline that she will marry James (Jimmy) Pazos in one month's time. At 37 years of age, Jimmy is 16 years her senior. The two meet only twice before the day of their simple ceremony in Pauline's Theo Georgios' and Thea Sophia's home.

Sophia, insisting that Pauline wear a western wedding gown, dresses her in a white, floor-length, velveteen dress with a lace-trimmed veil. She is handed a bouquet of two dozen white roses tied with ribbons and bits of greenery that trail down the front of her dress. It is the first time anyone has ever given Pauline flowers, and it seems an uncomfortable extravagance. The wedding party is made up of Theo Georgios and Thea Sophia, their two daughters, eleven-year-old Xeni, nine-year-old Esther, and the bridal couple's *Koumbaro* and *Koumbara*, (best man and his wife) Constantine and Chrysanthi Economu (shortened from Economopoulos). It is a small, traditional Greek wedding.

Standing before the priest in front of immediate family members, Jimmy and Pauline hold two large, lighted candles, symbolizing the light of Christ that is entering their lives. The couple is then given a goblet of wine from which they each take three sips; the prime number representing the indivisibility of their union, the wine symbolizing life and the communal sips, the sharing of their two lives. Next, the *Koumbaro* crowns the couple with the Greek *Stefana*, two beaded crowns joined together with a single satin ribbon, a physical representation of the joining of their two lives into one. The *Koumbaro* stands behind the couple and simultaneously switches the circlets three times back and forth between Pauline's and Jimmy's heads, symbolizing how they will reign over their household together. The candles and wine goblet are placed on the altar, around which the priest leads the newly crowned and beribboned couple three times. This is their first walk together as husband and wife representing their commitment to stay with each other throughout life's journeys. No vows are exchanged. The priest blesses the couple, removes the *Stefana*, and the ceremony is complete. Two photos are taken of the wedding party, followed by the standard Sunday dinner with the regular guests.

Xeni, James and Pauline Pazos, Cousin Pete,
Sophia and Georgios Athanasoulis

Pauline packs her three, hand-sewn dresses and a smattering of belongings into a single suitcase and moves out of Theo Georgios' house. The newly married Mr. and Mrs. James Pazos drive three hours northwest to their new home in Toledo where Pauline sleeps in a bed for the first time in 10 years. Her new home is already furnished thanks to the help of a female friend of Jimmy's. And although the furnishings are beautiful, Pauline struggles with a mixture of jealousy over the woman's involvement and guilt, knowing she should be grateful to have such a well-furnished home of her own. And while she is well prepared to assume the efficient running of her new household, she is wholly unprepared for the more intimate responsibilities of a wife, but this is nothing new. Thea Sophia has been negligent in sharing even the most basic womanly information with her niece.

As a young girl, Pauline is terrified by the onset of her menstrual cycle. She is bleeding and she doesn't understand why. Images of the two Ellis Island janitors, spitting *blood* into spittoons race to the forefront of her mind, and the only logical correlation emerges…. she must be dying of a similar disease. A pandemonium of questions and thoughts fill her head: *Am I going to bleed to death? Will I die tonight? What did I do to cause this? Thea is going to be angry.*

Frightened, Pauline does what makes perfect sense to a self-sufficient, 12 year-old girl. She stoically tamps down her fears and quietly takes care of herself. This is something at which she excels, and the business of it calms her. She covertly gathers cleaning rags to staunch the flow of blood and washes them out in secret at night. She frets and says fervent prayers before bed in case she doesn't wake in the morning. Her "condition" improves for a time only to return a month later, and her fretting and ministration start anew.

~ ~ ~

Pauline enters into her marriage with much the same benightedness. She knows people marry and have children, but is not cognizant of how this comes to be. A middle-aged Greek woman, a stranger, pulls her aside after her wedding ceremony and cryptically instructs her to let her new husband *"do whatever he wants in the bedroom."* Jimmy is patient for several weeks as Pauline comes to terms with the expectations of her new role as a wife.

CHAPTER 6

NEWS FROM ACROSS THE ATLANTIC

News from Lafka trickles in from time to time. Pauline's younger sister Demitra eventually bears three daughters, Vasiliki (Kiki), Konstantina (Deanna) and Athanasia (Soula). More *drachmas* cement Pauline's favorite sister Tasia's marriage to Georgios Barges. He is a good man, but his leg is badly injured a year after their marriage, fighting the Axis' occupation of Greece during the Greek Resistance Movement (1941 -1944). He is permanently disabled, shifting the physical field work to Tasia, her extended family and eventually their daughter Chrísanthi (Chrisa) and son Panagiotis (Taki) when they are old enough.

Adding to the family's hardships, Dimetra's husband Leonidas dies unexpectedly in 1952, leaving her to raise their three young girls. A short time later, their house burns to the ground, forcing them to move in with Tasia and Georgios and their two young children. The newly blended household of seven live off their land and what crops they can coax from it.

Word also reaches Pauline that her mother's niece, Christina Barbopoulus, Pauline's first cousin, is steaming to America by ship to become a *picture bride* to a Greek-American immigrant. She is to marry Theodore Alexopoulos, Americanized to Alex, whose family is from Gyoza, a village higher up in the mountains from Pauline's village. These arranged marriages are a burgeoning practice between poor, young Greek girls and estranged Greek men working far from home. Photographs are exchanged and marriages are negotiated long distance. In place of dowries, monies are scraped together by struggling brides' families for transatlantic tickets and temporary living expenses until their daughters can be married.

Christina arrives in New York City only to be met by Theodore Alex, *the imposter,* a much older, less attractive and more controlling man than the kind, handsome young stranger pictured in the photo. Like many women before her, she has been duped.

"I didn't want to marry him," Christina confided much later in life, "but he pleaded with me, saying I would humiliate him if I rejected him. I held out for two weeks until my small dowry ran out. Rejecting him would have embarrassed both of us...as well as our families. Besides, what other prospects did I have?" She offers with her signature shrug of stoicism.

Christina and Theodore Alex marry, settle in New York City and have two girls, Eiríni and Zoe and two sons George and Kosta, but she soon discovers her already *not so picture perfect groom* is also a serial philanderer.

Like many Greek immigrants, the couple operates a small restaurant below their second story apartment. When Christina ventures down to the restaurant after closing one evening, she finds her husband in the store room *in flagrante* with one of their waitresses. Dumbstruck by what she walks in on, she admonishes him with a comedic twist of words, "Wait until you finish, then I'll tell you a thing or two!"

But throughout their fifty-year marriage, she chooses to focus on the bright side and holds fast to her sunny, fun-loving personality. Maybe it is her talisman...or perhaps her passive act of defiance.... that she will not allow herself to be beaten down.

"He wasn't a good husband," she said sometime after his death, "but he gave me four beautiful children."

And there it is...*Timshel,* the Hebrew word that reminds us all that we possess the innate power to *choose*: between *poor me* or *lucky me*...between *happiness* or *misery*...between *honorable* or *evil.*

Christina and Pauline were young brides with similar outlooks on life, and the two remained close throughout their lives and hardships.

A Family Of Her Own
(Toledo, Ohio - 1930's)

Pauline experiences her first increments of freedom as a newly married woman to a social, charismatic and ambitious man. Over the next nine years, she and Jimmy welcome three daughters: Angie, Joanne and Tina. Pauline initially stays at home to raise their girls and keeps an immaculate house… without an oppressive taskmaster for the first time. Her attention is focused on the full time care of her children as well as the Herculean efforts to transform an abandoned fixer-upper into a loving home. She focuses her initial efforts on making it weatherproof. She repairs the broken and binding windows and doors, mends or replaces torn screens and refurbishes the storm windows she discovers in the rafters of their detached garage. Once the windows are back in working order, she gives them a thorough sanding, cleaning and a fresh coat of white paint. Inside the house, she strips, sands and refinishes the wood floors. She hand-sands and paints every square inch of the neglected plaster walls, ceilings and trim. Ever frugal and resourceful, she combines several open gallons of paint that she also finds in the garage to paint the interior walls and splurges on white enamel for the interior trim.

HERCULES
THE ROMAN NAME FOR THE GREEK DIVINE HERO HERACLES, WHO WAS THE SON OF ZEUS AND THE MORTAL ALCMENE. IN CLASSICAL MYTHOLOGY, HERCULES IS FAMOUS FOR HIS STRENGTH AND FOR HIS NUMEROUS FAR-RANGING ADVENTURES.

"I vividly remember our mother putting the heavy storm windows in place each fall," recalls Pauline's oldest daughter Angie. "She would man-handle the heavy panels down from the rafters in the garage, wash them and carry them one by one into the house. She refused to let us help. 'Too dangerous,' she would say. Then she would sit backward on the window ledge with her upper body outside the house, bracing her thighs against the sashes, so she wouldn't tumble out while maneuvering the heavy wood frames through the window opening, onto her lap, then up onto the hooks on the exterior brick above each window. It was a feat to behold, one that set our nerves on edge, especially when she progressed to the second story. She was strong and stubborn. It still unnerves me to picture her balancing on the window ledge two and a half floors above our concrete driveway."

Inside their new home, Pauline keeps an immaculate and well-decorated home, frequently rearranging the furniture, along with the rugs and furniture Brother Pete and Cousin Pete contribute for their second floor bedrooms. Pauline cooks, cleans and does the laundry for her family of five and their two, rent-free boarders.

She sews slipcovers for the upholstered furniture and two sets of curtains for each room, so the decor can be changed and cleaned twice a year. Outside, Pauline clears the neglected property of litter and debris and slowly, over time, fills in a large swale that runs the full length of the lot. Her efforts transform the blighted land into a lush, level yard, bordered entirely by well-tended vegetable and flower gardens. She sews clothes for herself and her girls and refinishes a set of rusty patio tables and chairs. Every possession serves a purpose and is meticulously maintained. Life centers around simple activities and fresh, home cooked food. The family's economical living allows them to send surplus dollars back to their families in Greece. Jimmy takes great pride in Pauline and her strong work ethic and surprises her on occasion with a small gift or outing. But with the approach of the Great Depression, even these small luxuries must be abandoned.

The White Star

Meanwhile, back at The Club Cafe, business is good. But after years of hard work, Mike, Uncle Nick and Brother Pete begin taking their earnings to New York to drink, gamble and blow off steam. During their absences, business at the restaurant takes a wild ride along with the restaurant's profits. Jimmy does his best to maintain the front end, but he is also drinking…in secret. The brothers' vices, coupled with the rising and falling revenues, become flash points for heated arguments. Mike and Nick continue their disappearing acts. The effort required to pick up the slack, coupled with the challenges of meeting payroll during the depression strains the partners' relationships and frustrates Jimmy. Before long, tempers boil over when Jimmy opens the restaurant safe to make payroll and discovers a substantial sum of money missing. In its place is a small box from a jewelry store, and in it, a diamond ring. He learns his Cousin Pete, the *Koumbaro* (Best Man) in a friend's upcoming wedding, plans to give it as a lavish wedding gift.

"I thought the bride should have a nice ring," Cousin Pete explains defensively to Jimmy with a dismissive shrug.

It is the straw that breaks the camel's back. The audacity of his cousin, using the restaurants money without asking, especially during difficult times, so enrages Jimmy that he calmly places the ring box on the counter, opens the cash register, extracts a $100 bill, plucks his hat from the coat rack and walks out of The Club Cafe…. for good.

He and Cousin Pete have been equal financial partners since The Club's inception. Each has invested years of hard work and most of their profits, but in Jimmy's anger, disgust and pride, he leaves it all behind. Everything. And so, in 1937, in the midst of the The Great Depression, Jimmy and Pauline begin a new life with only $100 to show for their entire life's work. Cousin Pete moves out of their home, and the couple uses their small personal nest egg, painstakingly put aside to purchase a foreclosed and abandoned gas station a short distance from their home. Pauline's hard work transforming their abandoned house gives Jimmy the confidence that they can successfully renovate the dilapidated gas station into a respectable diner.

With little other choice, Jimmy and Pauline roll-up their sleeves and get to work. They cover the oil changing pit with a wooden floor and install a no-frills lunch counter with floor mounted, swiveling bar stool seating. Jimmy's reputation and strong relationships within the restaurant industry help him secure lines of credit to purchase used kitchen equipment, plates, glasses, silverware, tables, chairs and food to stock the restaurant pantry. Like her childhood home in her family's village in Zevgolatio, Pauline paints the building white. She uses her sewing skills gleened from Mrs. White to make curtains, tablecloths and napkins out of red and white checkered fabric. They name their new restaurant *The White Star* in honor of

The White Star shipping line that brought both of them safely across the Atlantic.

When an estimate for a modest lighted sign comes in at $250, Jimmy approaches his long time house guest for a loan. Pete tells Jimmy that he just spent his remaining cash on a painting for his fiancé and can't help him out. Next, Jimmy and Pauline brave a trip to Newark to request a loan from Pauline's Theo Georgios, but Georgios Athan's cash is tied up in a new home he recently purchased for Sophia.

"If you had been here yesterday," Georgios tells Jimmy and Pauline, "I could have given you the money."

With no other choice, the couple make do with what they have. They hand letter *The White Star* in red paint over the dilapidated gas station sign and open their new restaurant for business. It is a humbling transition for Jimmy to open a simple diner on the outskirts of town and a modest beginning during difficult economic times to say the least. But Jimmy, like Pauline's cousin Christina, chooses to focus on the positive of owning and managing his own restaurant. He rises before dawn, making the short walk to The White Star to prep food and begin cooking. Pauline spends the early mornings feeding and dressing their two young daughters, Angie and Joanne, before joining Jimmy at 11:00 a.m. to help with the lunch service. And just like the difficult times in Greece, the couple makes sure no resources are wasted. They make the pies and baked goods from scratch each day. Jimmy dresses down whole sides of meat into roasts, steaks and chops. Pauline peels sacks of potatoes and turns pan drippings into rich gravies.

After the lunch rush, Jimmy walks home to take a nap. Their two girls stay with Pauline as she preps and bakes food for the dinner crowd. Jimmy returns at 4:30 p.m. to help cook and serve the food and serve beer and wine until closing at 2:00 a.m. The couple maintain these hours Monday through Saturday, closing the diner only on Sundays. When their two young girls are not in school, they are at the restaurant, playing store in the large, walk-in pantry, cutting out paper dolls and exercising their imaginations. When they grow tired, they cover themselves with beach towels and take naps in the backseat of the family car, parked just outside the front kitchen window where Pauline can keep an eye on them.

One afternoon while Angie and Joanne are at school and Pauline is alone at the restaurant, she climbs a ladder in the pantry to retrieve two large cans of tomatoes from the top shelf. As she shifts to counterbalance their weight, she slips off the ladder, and falls through a trapdoor to the former oil changing bay, landing hard on her right leg. No one is there to hear her cries, so she does what she has always done. She takes care of herself. A regular patron arrives as she is pulling herself up the stairs. He drives her to the nearby hospital where her broken leg is set and cast. She stays home for a few days while her girls do their best to help their father run the restaurant. They wrap silverware in napkins like their mother did when she was a young girl, portion pats of butter onto waxed paper squares and wait tables. But Pauline quickly returns to work, scooting around on her good leg while resting her casted leg on the seat of a chair. Life just goes on.

As The Depression deepens and World War II approaches, meat and sugar are rationed, forcing Jimmy and Pauline to close the restaurant early at 3:00 p.m. To reflect the change in hours, they rename the restaurant the White Star Lunch. But before long, even their lunch business tapers off.

"Times were hard, and although we may not have been rich, mom and dad made sure we were never hungry," recalls daughter Angie. "Many families ran low on food, but we always had the extra rations from the restaurant to help carry us through The Depression."

Newark Revisited

As the girls grow older, Pauline begins taking them to Newark for 1-2 weeks each summer to spend time with their second cousins, Xenia, Esther, Angel and their parents, Theo Georgios and Thea Sophia. They are, after all, the only family Pauline and her girls have in America. Angie and Joanne, like all growing seedlings, are tall and spindle-like. Sophia takes exception to this and bribes them to eat, offering to buy them new dresses if they gain two pounds during their stay. Their Theo Georgios even takes the girls to the drug store for milkshakes mixed with raw eggs for extra calories.

"Thea Sophia insisted we were skinny because we had worms," recalls Angie. "She even gave us worm medicine to help correct 'the problem'."

Sam Athan, a distant Newark relative, ups Sophia's ante, offering a new pair of shoes if the girls gain *more* than two pounds. He introduces them to their first hamburgers at Theo Georgios' Natoma Cafe in Newark. Angie and Joanne return home in their new dresses and shoes…and just as quickly, shed their unnatural weight.

One summer, after dropping her girls off in Newark, Pauline decides to make an impromptu stop in the small town of Shelby on her way back to Toledo. She exits OH-61, turns right onto West Main Street, and it's as if the physical landmarks, stalwart after two decades, rise up to greet her like old friends; Theo Georgios' old house, The Crystal Restaurant…even the doorway where her father hid her as a little girl on that cold January night…still recognizable. And she can't help herself. She parks her car in front of the old millinery shop across the street from the restaurant and walks up the stairs to the apartment that was the salvation of her terribly homesick, nine-year-old self some twenty-years ago.

She becomes smaller with each step, the familiar scent of the building, the same creaks in the wooden stair treads, but this time, the apartment number is no longer above her head, but at eye level. She raises her hand, knocks and pulls it quickly back to her chest to quiet her pounding heart. A stranger opens the door with a questioning look on her face. Pauline's bubble of hope pops. She recalibrates, introduces herself and inquires after the previous tenants. But the stranger isn't able to tell her anything about Mr. or Mrs. White. Then, a fleeting memory of Mr. White wearing a postal uniform stops Pauline's free fall. She asks the stranger if she can direct her to the town's post office. Once there, she goes to the counter and asks the postman on duty, "Is Mr. White here?"

The gray haired gentleman behind the counter says, "I'm Mr. White. Can I help you?"

Pauline takes a sharp intake of air as she realizes, *Of course he will be older now!* She recognizes him. Her heart rate quickens as she tentatively asks. "Do you remember me?"

The man's eyebrows knit together as he tries to place the visitor's face. "No, ma'am. I'm sorry. I don't."

"I'm Pauline…Panagiota Athanasouli," she says. I used to cut out paper dolls with your wife when I was a little girl. She taught me how to embroider."

Without taking his eyes off of Pauline, Mr. White tells his co-worker to take over his window. He disappears around the corner, bursts through the lobby door and lifts Pauline up into a big bear hug, spinning her in a joyous circle. When her feet are firmly rooted on the floor again, she tells him she is married and lives in Toledo with two beautiful daughters. Mr. White leads her to his home a short distance away to see his wife. When the two meet, there are more tears, hugs, stories, laughter…and such joy!

"I don't remember much about my drive back to Toledo," recalls Pauline decades later, "except I felt lighter. And just like when I was a homesick little girl in my Theo Georgios' car, I couldn't stop the tears from streaking down my face. But this time, they were very happy tears!"

There are angels who enter our lives and quietly leave behind gifts of immeasurable value. Mr. and Mrs. White provided Pauline with a sense of warmth and belonging all those years ago when she was so very far from home. Pauline drove away from their blissful reunion replenished with thoughts that centered her.

I existed!

I mattered!

They cared about me!

Sometimes one bright spark is all it takes to alter the course of someone's life.

Family Life

In 1940, Jimmy and Pauline welcome their third and final daughter Christina (Tina). The family of five speak Greek exclusively at home. Jimmy and Pauline place great importance on their girls' education, perhaps because it was something denied them. They send their girls to the nearby public grade

The Pazos family: Joanne, Pauline, Tina, Jimmy and Angie

school where all three learn to speak English for the first time. As part of their history and art curriculum, the girls take regular field trips to the nearby Toledo Art Museum. It has a profound and positive impact, instilling a lifelong appreciation of the arts. By age 12, Angie also shows a strong proficiency with numbers. She has more formal schooling as a seventh grader than both of her parents combined, so she is placed in charge of the White Star's finances.

When World War II is finally in the rearview mirror, the revenues from the restaurant begin to pick up, providing a modest, yet adequate living. Jimmy takes Pauline shopping, and despite her protests, buys her a brown mouton fur coat with a matching felt hat. It is the most extravagant gift Pauline has ever received. But it portends difficult times ahead.

Alcohol

As the U.S. economy rebounds after World War II, Jimmy and Pauline expand the White Star's operating hours. Jimmy's secretive drinking, exacerbated by recent economic challenges, begins to spill over into the family's home life. He gives up driving and arrives home uncharacteristically argumentative, demanding and intoxicated with greater frequency. Cousin Pete downplays his cousin's drinking, recounting childhood stories of finding Jimmy passed out behind wine barrels in Greece as a nine year old and excusing it as a *boys-will-be-boys* phase that will pass with time, which of course, it doesn't.

"I was 10 or 11 when I first remembered seeing my dad stay home from work," recalls Angie. "Mom would say 'Daddy is sick,' but beyond that, there would be no further explanation. We didn't talk about it. Having a problem with alcohol was bad enough. Acknowledging it to anyone else was shameful and embarrassing. Looking back, I realize Mom expended a lot of energy not only taking care of daddy but also protecting his image. But at home, we all knew he wasn't well."

A few days before Christmas in 1947, Jimmy hands Angie, Joanne and Tina some money and instructs them to go to the local dress shop and purchase the hostess dress in the front window that Pauline had been admiring. It will be his Christmas gift to her.

The girls' excitement grows as the sales clerk carefully folds and giftwraps the iridescent blue and purple gown in a large box with tissue paper and ties it up with a satin ribbon. The sisters race home with their package and place it carefully under the tree, bursting with excitement at the thought of their mother opening something so beautiful on Christmas morning!

When Jimmy doesn't come home at his usual time on Christmas Eve, Pauline and thirteen-year-old Angie walk to the restaurant to check on him while eleven-year-old Joanne watches her six-year-old sister Tina at the house. To their horror, Pauline and Angie find Jimmy passed out at the counter next to an empty liquor bottle purchased from a nearby store. The unlit gas jets on the commercial range are all on, though the exhaust fan is curiously also on. They immediately turn off the gas and open all the windows and doors. Angie stays with her father, while Pauline rushes home and returns with the family car. Mother and daughter then do their best to carry Jimmy's limp body out of the restaurant and into the back seat. When they get home, they reverse the process, carrying him out of the car, into the house and up a full flight of stairs to his bedroom. He recovers. The family goes ahead with their Christmas celebration the following morning, but the mood is subdued. Angie, Joanne and Tina open their gifts, but one present remains under the tree unopened. Over the next two weeks, it becomes the very large elephant in the room, before Pauline finally tells her daughters that they can open it and have whatever is inside.

When Jimmy is sober, he is a good husband and father, a fun-loving brother and cousin and an excellent businessman. He is intelligent, hardworking, personable and generous. He loves his wife and three little girls. But when he begins drinking, he finds it impossible to stop. He becomes his own worst enemy. For his family, it is a life filled with ups, downs and a great deal of uncertainty.

In 1948, the Pazos family takes a rare family vacation, a cross country road trip from Ohio to California. Pauline does all the driving along Route 66, stopping at night to sleep in the car, or in one of the rangy motels along the way. Since air conditioning doesn't become widely available in production cars until 1953, the family's only relief from the searing heat of Death Valley is the hot air blowing through their open windows. Thirteen-year-old Joanne entertains herself by holding her colorful, new scarf out the window to watch it flutter brilliantly in the breeze. But in the blink of an eye, it is ripped from her grasp by the envious dessert air. The three girls shriek as they look back and watch the scarf take flight above the road behind them.

"What's the matter?! What happened?!" A startled Pauline asks, her eyes flashing to the rear view mirror.

"Joanne was just holding her scarf out the window just like this," Angie explains, demonstrating with her own brightly colored scarf, when it too is torn from her fingers. This starts the family on a hysterical laughing jag, and the story becomes one of the more humorous highlights of the trip. Once they arrive in California they visit Knotts Berry Farm in Buena Park and stay with Constantino and Chrysanthi Economou in West Hollywood, the best man from their wedding and daughter Angie's Godparents. It is a happy and memorable vacation.

But as soon as they return home, Jimmy begins drinking his way to the bottom of 1-2 bottles of port wine each day. Pauline arrives with greater frequency at the White Star to an empty cash register… and Jimmy nowhere to be found. She doesn't hear from him for a few days…a week…sometimes a month until their hard earned money runs out. At times he comes home on his own, but increasingly Pauline receives desperate calls and dutifully retrieves her husband from sordid parts of town, unwashed, wearing the same clothes, still inebriated, but conscious enough to be a remorseful, emotional mess; crying and apologizing profusely and promising he will never drink again. The first few times, she believes him.

"If you've never grown up in a family with an alcoholic, you really can't grasp the uncertainty and anxiety it causes," recalls Angie. "When we were little, mom would tell us *'Baba* is sick'. As we got older, we realized he was a ticking time bomb of contradictions; a loving father…an embarrassing alcoholic; a successful, charismatic business owner…a detoxing drunk; an angry husband who would sometimes lash out in his frustration…and a remorseful man who was being swallowed up by personal demons. We never knew which person we would encounter from one day to the next. Inviting friends over was out of the question. My father's alcoholism was an embarrassing secret to be kept at all costs."

And just like all *secrets* it exacts a heavy toll on those tasked with keeping them. Pauline hunkers down, works harder and directs her energies toward The White Star and her three daughters. She pinches pennies to rebuild a secret cache of $2,500; a sizable sum in the late 1940's.

"I remember a heated exchange between my parents when I was about 17," recalls Angie. "More money was missing from the restaurant, and *Baba* was drinking heavily. I could smell the alcohol on him that day. I was standing in the corner of the living room and remembered seeing his suitcase on the floor next to him. My mom and dad argued openly, something I seldom witnessed."

"My mom rarely expressed her emotions, but that was all about to change. As the argument continued, mom's pent up anger and frustration reached its tipping point. She threw a glass bottle of Coca-Cola against the wall between the living room and the front hallway. I remember the bottle breaking through the plaster and lodging in the lathe, where it remained miraculously unbroken. Then my dad grabbed her and started shaking her. I stepped between them like a referee and told him to stop. He did and my mom ran upstairs."

"Call me a taxi!" Jimmy barks at his daughter. "I'm leaving!"

"Where do you want to go, *Baba?*" Angie asks, trying to calm him down, "I can drive you."

"Take me to the Secor Hotel!" He demands.

Before Angie and her father can leave, Pauline rushes back into the room, throwing her wedding ring, watch and $2,500 in small bills and saving bonds on the floor in front of her husband of 19 years.

"Here! Take it! Take it all, and GO!" She seethes. "I don't want anything from you except the house to raise the kids in."

Jimmy is taken aback. He is unaccustomed to an outburst like this from Pauline. He hesitates before bending down and scooping up the money, leaving her watch and ring on the floor before stalking out the front door. He gets into the family car, and Angie drives him the short distance to the Secor Hotel in downtown Toledo.

Early the next morning, after a sleepless night, Pauline runs down the block to Jimmy's brother's house and pounds urgently on the door.

"What is it, Panagiota?" George's wife Helen asks as she opens the door, still pulling on her robe and setting her hair in order.

"I need to talk to George right away!" Pauline tells her sister-in-law. "Wake him, and tell him to meet me at the restaurant!"

"What is it, Panagiota? What's going on?" George asks as he joins his wife at the front door in an undershirt and hastily donned trousers.

"Jimmy is drinking again," she tells them self consciously. "He got angry and left the house last night! Angie took him to the Secor Hotel." Pauline hesitates before continuing, "He took a lot of money with him. I need you to go to the hotel and bring him back before it's all gone."

"Of course!" George reassures her "But I have to go to The Club Cafe until the lunch crowd leaves. I'll go right after that."

"No! You have to go now!" Pauline pleads in desperation. "He won't be there later!"

As a compromise, George calls the Secor Hotel and miraculously reaches Jimmy who promises to meet him in the lobby of the hotel at 1:00 p.m., but when George arrives, Jimmy is already checked out.

The Copper Queen
(1950)

Four days later, the doorman at The Copper Queen Hotel in Bisbee, Arizona, watches as an intoxicated, disheveled man weaves his way toward the hotel, loses his balance on the front steps and tumbles down into the dusty street. The doorman rushes over to help the man who is semi-conscious and mumbling in what sounds like a foreign language.

The man is too drunk to be taken in among the hotel guests, so the doorman enlists the help of a bellman to carry him up to a bench on the side of the hotel. Next, he places a call to the local mayor.

"Hi, Angelo?" The doorman says. "It's Luke up at The Copper Queen, I have a fellow here who is in trouble. I can't understand a word he is saying. I think he might be one of your people. Come down here and give me a hand! Quickly!"

When Angelo arrives, he confirms that the man is indeed speaking in Greek and is further shocked to come face-to-face with his *first cousin Jimmy Pazos*. He looks him over for injuries and finds a large sum of money and some bonds in the breast pocket of his rumpled jacket. Jimmy is in such deplorable condition that Angelo takes him to the local hospital. He informs the hospital staff that he will cover Jimmy's expenses and instructs them to let their new patient make a long distance phone call to his home when he sobers up. Later that day, four and a half days after Jimmy's abrupt departure, the phone rings at Pauline's home. A still intoxicated Jimmy is on the phone with an angry message.

"I am in Arizona," he stammers with difficulty. "I don't want anything from you but the underwear I'm wearing! In a few days you'll get a letter from a lawyer for a divorce!" The call abruptly ends.

Not knowing what to do, Pauline talks with Jimmy's Cousin Pete. "Jimmy just called. He is in Arizona! What should I do?"

"He is sick," replies Cousin Pete. "You need to go to Arizona and help him. He has a cousin named Angelo Rojokos who lives there. Here's his phone number. Call him, and he will help you."

Pauline places a call to Angelo Rogokos to explain her predicament and make travel plans. To her surprise, Angelo already knows of Jimmy's transcontinental trip. He is the town's Mayor, who was called to help him. He fills her in on Jimmy's current condition and assures her that he will take good care of him, and that she needn't make the arduous trip.

"I'll watch over him while he is in Bisbee," he tells Pauline by phone. "He's in bad shape, but he is in the hospital now and will be better in a few days. He had a lot of money with him when I found him. I want you to know that I put it in my safe. When he is well, I will use part of it to buy a train ticket back to Toledo, then I'll wrap him up like a *Koufeto* (box of candy) and send him and the money safely back to you."

Several days later, when Jimmy has dried out, Angelo books his train ticket to Toledo. He calls Pauline as promised, gives her Jimmy's arrival date and time and personally sees his cousin onto the train. As the two men part ways, Angelo hands Jimmy the envelope with the remaining $2,200 in cash and bonds and wishes him a safe trip home. But when Pauline arrives at the train station in Toledo on the appointed date and time, Jimmy is nowhere to be found.

He started drinking again during a brief stopover in Chicago, forgetting or foregoing the final leg of his trip. He continues his bender in the Windy City for another week until the remaining money is exhausted. Then the familiar cycle repeats; a desperate phone call to Pauline for help, a frightening drive to a shabby location, a filthy, guilt-ridden and remorseful husband and an attempt by both to re-enter a life to which neither can relate.

"When we had dinner guests at the house, it was customary to serve a shot of Greek Ouzo or whiskey after dinner," recalls Angie. "I guess I was a resentful teen because I used to place the filled glasses on a try and serve each guest individually, purposefully saving the very last glass for my dad. Because he never drank in front of people, he would make a spectacle of taking a microscopic sip, puckering his face as if it is the most distasteful liquid he had ever consumed and handing the unfinished shot back to me. It was a spiteful thing to do on my part, but it gave me a perverse sense of enjoyment to see the discomfort it caused him."

Jimmy's alcoholism continues to spiral. On a particularly cold winter evening, Pauline discovers him passed out in a snowbank outside their home. His body is frigid and stiff. Her adrenaline kicks in, and she manages to single handedly drag him up the steps on their front porch, a full flight of stairs to a warm bath to raise his body temperature and then into his bed to sleep it off.

In the spring, when the snow melts, the evidence of Jimmy's prodigious drinking is revealed. Angie, Joanne and Tina watch from a second story window as their mother picks up bushel baskets of empty liquor bottles he has tossed into the snow banks between the house and The White Star. At the height of Jimmy's drinking he attempts to break down Pauline's bedroom door with a crowbar. For the next several nights, Pauline sleeps in the backseat of their car with the doors locked. She eventually makes a desperate call to Jimmy's brother George in Dayton. When he comes to Toledo and sees Jimmy's condition, he gently tells Pauline, "We have to get him some help at a hospital, Panagiota."

"But how will I run the restaurant?" She asks. "What will people think?"

Her daughter Angie is present and brazenly interjects, "Mom, what do you think people will think when they see him stumbling home drunk or passed out in the street?"

Pauline is hesitant at first, but George gives her the courage and *permission* she needs to finally commit Jimmy to a psychiatric hospital for treatment of his alcoholism. He also assures Pauline that he will stay to help her run The White Star while Jimmy recovers. That same day, Jimmy is traumatically removed from the house in a straight jacket. Visitation by the family is prohibited for several weeks as he detoxes. After 60 days, he is released to a transitional community where he lives for another month with fellow recovering alcoholics. The men maintain their own cottages and offer support to one another. Jimmy becomes a model resident and wins competitions for maintaining the best flower and vegetable gardens. He eventually returns to Pauline and The White Star, but every now and then, he preemptively packs his bags, telling Pauline, "I think I need to go back" (to the transitional community)", which he does on several occasions, staying until his body's tremendous urge for alcohol passes.

ALCOHOLISM IS AN INSIDIOUS
MONSTER THAT WAITS PATIENTLY
FOR THE SLIGHTEST SIGN OF WEAKNESS;
RETURNING TO SWALLOW ITS VICTIMS
WHOLE WHEN THEY LEAST EXPECT IT.
– MAREN WALKER

One year later, in 1951, Pauline receives word that her Theo Georgios has died. The news stirs a maelstrom of unexpected emotions. She gathers her family and drives to Newark to attend the funeral of the man who was married to a woman who was demanding and unkind to her. When she walks up to her uncle's coffin to pay her final respects, all the difficult memories and unshed tears from her childhood well-up and burst their dam. She slumps against the casket, sobbing uncontrollably; not for her uncle, but for the loss of her mother, her family and her childhood. Seventeen-year-old Angie gently pulls her mother away, ushering her to a quiet corner of the church to compose herself.

The rush of emotion takes even Pauline by surprise. A family friend from Newark several years older than Pauline suddenly materializes at her side like an apparition. George Brown offers his condolences, and the two talk…and talk…and talk. He shares his memories of the day Pauline arrived at The Crystal Restaurant as a lost little girl from Greece. He tells her stories of watching her grow up, sensing the falseness of Sophia's carefully constructed facade and witnessing the difficulties and injustices she inflicted on Pauline. He validates Pauline.

"Someone else saw it…"

"I didn't imagine it!"

And a warm feeling of peace and closure settles gently over her.

Angelike

Angie graduates from high school and expresses a desire to attend a four-year college, but it is a costly proposition for Jimmy and Pauline. The three reach a hard fought compromise. Angie will attend a business school while living at home. Two years later, a Toledo entrepreneur calls the school asking them to send out their best candidate to interview for an accounting/office manager position at his plastics business. Angie Pazos arrives on time for the interview, but the business owner is out. She settles in to wait. Two hours later, Richard (Dick) Schreder returns, having completely forgotten about the interview. He hires Angie on the spot in what will turn out to be one of his best business…and personal decisions.

Despite Dick being married and an 18 year age difference, he and his new office manager find common ground running the business, bonding over their respective families' grocery and restaurant businesses…and alcoholic fathers. Before long, the two begin secretly dating. As Angie primps for one of their clandestine meetings, the pieces of a troublesome puzzle click into place for Pauline; a worrisome image for any parent, but a particularly devastating one for the first born daughter of a Greek family. She confronts Angie, and the two exchange heated words. Pauline forbids her from leaving the house, but Angie moves defiantly toward the bedroom door. Their raised voices bring Jimmy up from the living room, calling for "Quiet!".

"I was a headstrong twenty-year-old who happened to fall in love with the trifecta of Greek '*No-No's*'. Dick was not Greek. He was married, and he was much older than me. Looking back, I can understand my parents' concern."

Two years later, in 1957, after Dick's divorce, he and Angie marry in a small civil ceremony at his Toledo home. Angie's sisters attend, but Joanne declines Angie's invitation to be her maid of honor. The arrival of her cousins Xenia and Esther and their families brings bittersweet tears of appreciation to Angie's eyes. But her parents remain noticeably absent.

(L to Rt) Richard, Angie, Pastor,
best man Francis Holmes, sister Tina.

"I put my parents through a lot in the years leading up to our marriage," says Angie. "If I had been more forthright and patient, allowing everyone to grow more comfortable with our relationship, maybe I could have had the support of my entire family at my wedding."

The decision not to attend her own daughter's wedding could not have been an easy one for Pauline who knew first hand what it was like to wed without her own parents present…albeit for different reasons. After a two month estrangement from Angie, Pauline quietly extends an olive branch. She wraps a belated wedding gift and places it inside the front storm door of Angie and Dick's new home.

"Unfortunately, we never used our front door," recalls Angie. "I didn't find her package for almost two weeks, but when I did, I cried and called her immediately. And just like that, our rift was mended!"

Joanne

When Joanne graduates high school, she has an easier time convincing her parents to send her to college. She attends Ohio State University, earns a degree in interior design and falls in love with a young Greek-American named John Copetas from Pittsburgh. They become engaged and plan a springtime wedding. They also make preparations to serve alcoholic beverages at their reception.

"Our Dad had been sober for some time," says Angie, "but I felt the alcohol might pose too big a temptation for him, and I spoke out against it."

John and Joanne's wedding plans continue. Alcohol is served, and Jimmy falls off the wagon again at his daughter's wedding reception. And as if this is not difficult enough, a few months later, Pauline receives a telegram from her mother in Greece.

Thanasios and Kostandina Athanasoulis

Dear Panagiota,

I write to tell you that your father has died. He died of a broken heart because he left you in America and never saw you again. Please come home to visit. I have forgotten what you look like.

Mama

...H-e d-i-e-d o-f a b-r-o-k-e-n h-e-a-r-t... Twenty simple letters.

Pauline is distraught. She had no knowledge of her father even being ill. She turns to Jimmy with shaking hands and asks, "What should I do?"

"You need to go home, Pauline," Jimmy tells her. "You need to spend time with your mother and sisters. Take as much time as you want. Tina can go with you, and I will take care of the restaurant. Everything will be fine."

RETURNING TO GREECE
Zevgolatio - 1957

Pauline plans her trip home for early summer. The restaurant is open for breakfast and lunch. Jimmy is sober and better able to manage the reduced hours alone. Angie and Joanne are married and well established in their own homes nearby. Tina, 17, accompanies her mother on a much shorter, eleven-day voyage across the ocean, *back* to Greece this time on an ocean liner named the Olympia.

OLYMPIA
ACCORDING TO ANCIENT GREEK
MYTHOLOGY, OLYMPIA IS THE HOME AND
SANCTUARY OF THE GOD ZEUS, THE GOD OF THE
SKY, LIGHTNING AND THE THUNDER IN ANCIENT
GREEK RELIGION AND LEGENDS, AND RULER
OF ALL THE GODS ON MOUNT OLYMPUS.

Pauline hasn't seen her mother, sisters or her village for nearly four decades. It feels surreal that she is suddenly able to go home again. Angie's husband Dick, an avid aviation enthusiast, flies his new mother and sister-in-law in one of his private planes to New York City. She and Tina take a taxi to the harbor and board the Olympia bound for Athens. As the two Pazos women stand on the top deck and the engines labor to get the ship underway, Pauline's thoughts flutter back to her previous trans-Atlantic trip.

A panoply of memories swirl through her mind as the Statue of Liberty bids them safe travels, and for the next 4,289 nautical miles, she exists in a state of duality, simultaneously experiencing herself as a nine-year-old child and a forty-seven-year-old woman.

Thirty-nine years ago, she traveled to America on the King Alexander as a little girl...to everything foreign. Today, she returns to her home in Greece as a married woman with three grown children...to everything that was once familiar....the comfort and security of her family and the love of her mother for which she has ached. It forces a reconciliation of confusing thoughts and emotions; different, yet painfully similar. Her father is not accompanying Tina and her this time, but she feels the closeness of his spirit guiding them home. And for the first time in her life, she realizes she is in control of her own destiny.

Eleven days later, as the ship approaches its destination, Pauline relives the excitement of passengers scrambling deck side to catch their first glimpse of the approaching harbor. Her adrenaline spikes as the speck on the horizon, Piraeus this time, not New York, grows in mass and sprouts buildings like the mythical city of Atlantis rising from the sea.

Greece!

Piraeus!

Home!

ATLANTIS

ACCORDING TO LEGEND, ATLANTIS CITY WAS BUILT BY POSEIDON – THE GREEK GOD OF SEA, OF STORMS AND EARTHQUAKES – WHEN HE FELL IN LOVE WITH A MORTAL WOMAN CLEITO. HE MADE THIS CITY ON TOP OF A HILL, ON AN ISOLATED ISLAND IN THE SEA, TO PROTECT HER AND NAMED IT ATLANTIS.

Her heart hammers excitedly in her chest...then just as quickly flip flops to a fear so primal, she has to hide her trembling hands.

Will they remember me?

Will I recognize them?

Will our house look the same?

Will I fit in?
Will I still belong

There are crowds of people at the Port of Piraeus, waving energetically as the ship's crew throw out mooring lines that are smartly snapped up and tethered to the bollards on the dock. As she and Tina disembark, Pauline scans the faces in the crowds below; not for Greek gods and goddesses this time, but for anyone familiar. Passenger names are announced as each party disembarks, gathers their baggage and is quickly enveloped by enthusiastic friends and relatives. Pauline is acutely attuned to any shouts that sound remotely like *"Pauline Pazos!"*, but she hears nothing. As the crowds thin, she asks a young baggage handler to call out her name again. He walks up and down the fence bellowing, "Pauline Pazos!"

No response.

"Pauline Pazos!"

Still nothing.

Then, a new thought occurs to her. "Try my maiden name, Panagiota Athanasouli!" She urges.

"Panagiota Athanasouli!" The boy dutifully calls out.

Still no response.

"Panagiota Athanasouli!"

Silence.

She and Tina are the last unclaimed passengers. She tamps down her fear and disappointment and retrieves a slip of paper from her purse with a phone number written on it; the first of a convoluted series of steps needed to reach her family in their remote village of Lafka. As she scans the dock area for a public telephone, she is suddenly swept into the embrace of a man with a large mustache who exclaims, *"Ω Θεέ μου! Νομίζαμε ότι το πλοίο σας έφτασε αύριο! Έφτασα εδώ όσο πιο γρήγορα μπορούσα!"* (Oh my God! We thought your ship arrived tomorrow! I got here as fast as I could!).

Pauline pushes the man abruptly away. *"Περίμενε ένα λεπτό! Ποιος είσαι;"* (Wait a minute! Who are you?).

"Είμαι ο κουνιάδος σου Φίλιπα! Ο άντρας της Ξένης!" (I'm your brother-in-law Phillipa! Xeni's husband! He says.

The rest of the story spills out as Phillipa gathers their luggage and directs Pauline and Tina to a waiting taxi. He is not taking them to Lafka to see her mother Kostandina. No. He is taking them to a nearby hotel where her mother and three sisters are anxiously awaiting her arrival. Pauline exhales, releasing a lifetime of tension. In its place, a mixture of feelings clamor to take its place: surprise, relief, excitement, joy, sadness, impatience, apprehension. She looks at her seventeen-year-old daughter, and pride piles onto her already raucous scrum of emotions. *Mama will finally see one of her American-born grandchildren!*

"Hurry, Phillipa! Tell the driver to hurry!" Pauline urges. She pulls Tina from the taxi almost before the car stops in front of the inn. They hurry inside as Phillipa shouts the room number after them and stays behind with their luggage. Pauline hurries to a door with the lucky number "3" on it. Her knuckles hover inches from it as an image of Mr. and Mrs. White's old apartment door plays through her mind.

In cardinal moments like this, time seems to expand. For the next few moments, Pauline registers everything in detached, slow motion: her uncertain rap and the pandemonium as the door is swept open: shouts, tears, hugs, shock and nervous laughter. Pauline and Tina are crushed by the occupants of the room, their Greek family members who are also strangers, but there is no one else in the world with whom Pauline would rather be.

Her mother can only cry, hugging Pauline and touching her face, her arms, her hands, again and again as if to reassure herself that her long absent daughter is not an apparition. It is a joyous reunion. Her daughter and one of her granddaughters are finally home! Phillipa and Kostandina, Pauline and Tina, Xeni, Dimetra, and Tasia immediately check out of the inn and climb into a waiting taxi to begin their two-hour trip to Tashia's village Zevgolatio. As they motor through the countryside, the relaxed atmosphere affords them time in which to become reacquainted. Pauline breathes deeply for the first time in what seems like decades and is richly rewarded with the familiar, velvety aromas that soothe her soul: freshly turned soil, wood smoke, oregano, garlic. And there is time to study her mother with cautious, stolen glances. She is seventy-six years old with long gray hair pulled back into a bun at the nape of her neck. It contrasts with the black clothes she now wears from head to toe, the uniform of all Greek widows, but its message is anything but benign. To Pauline, it seems to shout *Baba is dead!* with a finality that is sobering and disquieting. She can no longer pretend she will see her father when they get home. And other things have changed too. In Tasia's village where they are to be reunited with extended family members, Pauline doesn't recognize a single soul. Home and family are supposed to be familiar…only they aren't. Her sisters are married women with husbands and grown children she has never met.

Pauline and Tina stay in the home of Tasia, her youngest sister, and her husband Georgio and their two children, daughter Chrísa and son Taki. They live at the foot of the mountains in a single story concrete home that has electricity and a bit more room than their childhood home in Lafka which is another two hour drive further up the mountain. Although her sisters Xeni and Dimetra live in nearby Braiebe and Goura respectively, they stay with Pauline at Tasia's house for several days. Xeni remains aloof, and Pauline finds it difficult to connect with her. Dimetra is more welcoming, but with a personality that gravitates more toward pessimism. Pauline finds the most common ground with Tasia. She has an upbeat, contented disposition, and the two quickly find their sisterly bond.

After a few days, Xeni and Dimetra must return to their respective families, but Pauline's mother stays with Pauline and Tina at Tasia's house for the duration of their visit. Georgio, Tasia, Chrísa, Taki, Kostandina, Pauline and Tina settle into a rhythm, and before long, all things foreign become familiar. While there is electricity at her sister's house, there is still no running water or indoor plumbing. Water is brought from the well in buckets. Clothes are washed outside in the large stone basin, and food is still cooked in the same copper pots of her childhood in the traditional kiln-like oven over embers of grapevine trimmings.

Life in Lafka

After several weeks in Zevgolatio, it is time to travel to Pauline's childhood home in Lafka where they will see more extended family and friends Tasia's son Taki arranges for a taxi to drive Kostandina, Tasia, Pauline and Tina. They fit their small suitcases in the trunk and settle in for the two and a half hour drive. Automobiles are still an extravagance in the village in 1958. The road leading up the mountain is unpaved and rutted, but for the three women, it is a thoroughly enjoyable trip. The days leading up to this moment must have felt like a game of hot potato for Pauline as she moved *closer* and *hotter* to the epicenter of her previous life. As their taxi rounds the final line of tall Cypress trees bordering the road to her village, Pauline's hand flies to her mouth in shock, and she begins to cry.

The entire village of Lafka has turned out to welcome her home. Men, women and children line both sides of the dirt road. They clap and jump and shout as the taxi and its long-awaited occupants come into view. Pauline doubles over, covering her face with both hands, sits up, daring a second look, then doubles over again unaware of her own actions. Dimetra is the lone familiar face among the crowd, but the villagers all know Pauline. She is the spitting image of her late father Thanasi Athanasoulis. The village has savored every piece of information about her that trickled back to their ears from across the Atlantic.

In small communities, everyone knows everything about one another. Sadness is divided and happiness multiplied. News of Pauline's life in America helped lift the entire village over the years, but it never erased the sadness they felt over one of their seedlings being plucked from their soil all too early. Their turnout for Pauline's return is an unexpected, yet glorious welcome home. It is a revelation to her that her village also felt the loss of *her* leaving *them*. Her return is not only healing for Pauline but also for the entire village. A Greek proverb fills her thoughts with greater meaning:

"YOU HAVE TO HAVE STRONG ROOTS
TO WITHSTAND LIFE'S STORMS."

Returning to her roots is transformative. Pauline weathered a number of storms in America, yet she realizes for the first time that perhaps she did not do so alone. She persevered because of the foundational love and support of her family and the people of Lafka who sprinkled her childhood with all the essential nutrients to help her roots grow *deep* and *strong*.

As the taxi drives into the heart of the village, many of the buildings remain unchanged and a flood of early memories wash over her. She inhales deeply…then slowly releases her breath as the taxi comes to a stop in front of the stone house of her childhood; her *home*, with the same outlying structures, kiln, chicken coop and outdoor bathroom where she helped her three-year-old sister Tasia go potty so many years ago. She climbs out of the car without tearing her gaze from it, and with each step forward… travels backward in time. She drinks in her physical surroundings and the evocative scents that conjure deep seated memories of her mother, father, and her sisters and herself as young girls. Her face flushes with heat as her recollections of each tenderly curated moment are validated in emotional and sensory snap shots as if paging through a cherished photo album: the well, the stone wash tub, the smell of wood smoke, the copper cooking pots still hanging in the same spot on the kitchen wall, her old bed…and sadly, the family members who are absent; *Baba* and her siblings Spiro, Olga and the beautiful little Eleni.

She and Tina stay in Lafka for the final portion of their stay. The agriculturally-based life of Pauline's childhood continues virtually unchanged since 1919. Dimetra and her adult children still tend the crops in their respective families' fields. It's late June, and Tina watches her cousins (Dimetra's daughters) Vasiliki (Kiki), Deanna and Soula, harvest the golden stalks of wheat by hand. As one makes broad swipes with a hand-held scythe that cuts and lays the wheat neatly over on its side, the two other sisters follow behind to bundle the stalks into sheafs. They are left in the field for 10 days. Once dried and cured, they are piled in a circular depression in the earth, and a heavy wooden sled with metal threshing blades is placed on top.

"Tina joined us as we scrambled on top of the threshing sled, sitting side by side to weigh it down," Tina's older cousin Kiki later recalls. "The threshing was always a welcome reprieve from the physical labor of harvesting. A rope was tethered from the inside edge of our sled to a stake at the center of the bowl-shaped depression. Another rope was tied from the outside edge of our sled to two harnessed donkeys on the outer perimeter of the circle."

Kiki's mother Dimetra (Pauline's younger sister) grabs the reins of the lead donkey and slaps its hindquarter. "Let's go!" She shouts with authority.

The cousins' fun begins with jolts, bumps and lots of laughter as their sled is dragged over the undulating stalks of wheat; 'round and 'round, like the hands on the face of a clock, until the stalks are broken down and the hardened grain heads are separated from their stalks. Tina's cousins later toss baskets-full of the ground-up mixture into the air, allowing the heavier grain to drop straight down and the lighter chaff to flutter to the side. But in Greece, not even the chaff is wasted. It is gathered up for animal feed and bedding. Then Dimetra and her girls work side by side to scoop the valuable grain into fifty-pound, coarsely-woven bags that are tied shut and loaded onto the donkeys for the trek home, or to the flour mill. The process is repeated for several days until the entire field of wheat is cleared, cured, threshed and either stored or ground.

Pauline is taken aback by the physicality of the work. She pulls her one niece aside and says "Kiki, I feel terrible that you and your sisters have to work so hard."

"Take me to America, Thea!" Kiki implores her aunt Pauline. "I want to leave here!"

"There was so little future for us in Greece," recalls Kiki many years later. "It was a hard life. I was good at sewing, and while I worked in the fields, I dreamed of traveling to America to get married and become a seamstress."

Through Tina's Eyes

"It was an eye opening experience to live without electricity or running water," recalls Tina many years later. "When my cousins and the villagers would return from long days in the fields, they would gather at the spring-fed fountain in the village center to relax, then return to their home with heavy clay pots of water balanced on their heads or shoulders. They wouldn't let me help. The only thing I could do was try to use as little water as possible to reduce the number of their trips to the well."

The bathroom at Pauline's childhood home in Lafka is still the same small outbuilding with the open raftered roof adjacent to the chicken coop. But her father had upgraded it slightly after his final return from America with a porcelain toilet fixture, so his family wouldn't have to squat over the open hole in the ground.

"At night, when the moon set behind the mountain, the village sky would grow black as ink," recalls Tina. "We had to light a torch to find our way. I'll never forget the first time I had to go to the bathroom in the middle of the night. I didn't realize the chickens roosted in the open rafters of the shared roof after sunset. When I walked in, the flame from my torch startled them awake and into a squawking frenzy. Scared me half to death! After that, I made sure I went to the bathroom before I went to bed."

On Saturday evenings, the villagers gather in the square to visit over cups of strong Greek coffee, a glass of wine or sips of *Ouzo*, a licorice-flavored liqueur. On special occasions such as the the end of various harvests, Easter, weddings, or religious festivals, there would be *Bouzouki* music and traditional folk dancing. Tina's cousins invite her to join them for the wheat harvest celebration, but when Tina shows them the dress she packed, her cousins fall silent. Tina's dress is out of step with Greek fashion. Kiki takes her under her wing and uses her artistic eye and sewing skills to shorten and update it.

Over the next three months, Tina gets to know the young men and women of both Lafka and Zevgolatio at the various gatherings and boat rides across the nearby Gulf of Corinth. She becomes smitten with a young Greek man named Ulysseus Papalekas who lives conveniently close to Tasia's house in Zevgolatio, and before long, her Greek-American boyfriend back home is quickly forgotten.

"It was very romantic," recalls Tina. "There was a full moon on one particular boat ride, and I remember wearing a yellow chiffon dress with a scarf around my neck that trailed behind me in the wind. Just like in the movies!"

ULYSSES
A LEGENDARY GREEK KING OF ITHACA AND THE HERO OF HOMER'S EPIC POEM THE ODYSSEY. HUSBAND OF PENELOPE, FATHER OF TELEMACHUS, AND SON OF LAËRTES AND ANTICLEA.

As Tina socializes, Pauline stays as close to her mother as possible, attempting to fill the chasm created by almost four decades of separation. She helps her cook and do housework. One night as the two get ready for bed, Pauline says to her mother, *"Mama,* I missed you so much for so many years. Let me sleep in the same bed with you tonight."

Her mother self-consciously asks, "Why would you want to sleep with me? I am a smelly, old woman."

But none of that registers with Pauline as she lifts the covers and slides in next to her. She is in her home country with her mother, something she has yearned for every day since she was nine years old. They are finally reunited and breathing the same air as it was meant to be.

In the middle of the night, Pauline wakes to the shifting of the bed and watches her mother walk outside to the bathroom. She lays there waiting for her return, feeling the same emptiness in her mother's momentary absence as she experienced throughout her childhood. But instead of coming back to lie next to her daughter, Kostandina lays down in a separate bed for the remainder of the night. It must have seemed like a simple act on her part. For whether it assuaged Kostandina's physical discomfort, embarrassment or guilt, the act conveys a heart-rending message to Pauline…her mother's rejection.

Pauline pretends to be asleep as the hot, salty tears of her child-within run down the cheeks of a grown woman and pool in her ears. The wound in her heart, partially healed by their recent reunion, opens painfully back up. She spends the remainder of the night slowly folding her tattered emotions back into the safety of her innermost box. As a child in America, Pauline resisted the urge to look back at what could have been, to what she missed out on, but tonight, like the Greek poet Orpheus, Pauline looks back in an unguarded moment as the mother-daughter relationship she so craves slips slowly out of her reach.

ORPHEUS
A POET WHO WENT TO THE UNDERWORLD AFTER THE DEATH OF HIS WIFE EURYDICE AND SECURED HER RELEASE FROM THE DEAD, BUT LOST HER BECAUSE HE FAILED TO OBEY THE CONDITION THAT HE MUST NOT LOOK BACK AT HER UNTIL THEY REACHED THE WORLD OF THE LIVING.

Returning to America

After three months, Pauline and Tina's trip draws to a close. It is time for them to return to America. Although Pauline's original goal of recapturing the lost years with her mother remains elusive, she feels content. She leaves her mother and sisters, knowing she *can* and *will* return.

The trip is successful for Tina as well. She connects with the strength of her Greek roots as well as the eligible young Ulysseus. The two continue to communicate long distance, and their romance blossoms. Arrangements for their marriage are made one year later, but Tina develops a small case of cold feet. Her sister Joanne and husband John advise Tina that she is free to say "no". She asks her oldest sister Angie for her opinion.

Angie replies, *"You've seen how the women in Greece live. If you would be content living in the same manner, say 'yes'. If not, then say 'no'."*

Tina says 'yes', and Ulysseus travels to America to claim his bride. Jimmy and Pauline agree to sponsor and help establish him in a business. They also provide the newlyweds with a modest two-bedroom house located halfway between the White Star and the family's home on Haverfield Court in Toledo, Ohio. But when the couple's wedding license is posted in the paper, the immigration authorities show up on Angie and Dick's doorstep looking for Ulysseus. Dick is conveniently unable to provide them with any details on his whereabouts. It buys enough time for Tina and Ulysseus to be hastily married by a justice of the peace to forestall his deportation. Immigration officials return later that same day and pepper the newlyweds with personal questions to make sure their marriage is not one of "convenience". The couple commits a small lie, telling the authorities that their marriage has already been consummated. This declaration proves satisfactory. The officials depart, and a few days later, the couple is *officially* married in the Greek Orthodox Church.

Over the next six years, Jimmy and Pauline are blessed with six healthy grandbabies from their three daughters and sons-in-law. Sunday dinners at Jimmy and Pauline's house help keep the expanding families close. Pauline babysits for Tina's son Pano and sentimentally sews wardrobes for her granddaughters' collections of dolls. The grandkids spend weekends at their *YiaYia* and *Papou's* house, playing, swinging on the tire swing under an enormous oak tree and eating lunch at the White Star. Jimmy and Pauline's personal sacrifices and hard work greatly expanded the opportunities for their children and grandchildren, but the hardships of their extended families back in Greece were never far from their minds.

An Important Letter

The following Fall one year later, Kiki is once again working in the fields of Lafka, when her sister Deana runs towards her, waving a red, white and blue banded airmail envelope in the air.

"It's a letter for you from Thea Pauline in America!"

Kiki reaches excitedly for it, but Deanna pulls it out of her grasp. "How much will you give me for it?" She taunts.

Kiki curses her sister under her breath as she muscles it away and tears it open. Tears spring to her eyes at the sight of a check with the accompanying words… "Y-o-u-r p-a-s-s-a-g-e t-o A-m-e-r-i-c-a…" *Twenty Simple letters* with the power to finally make Kiki's dream a reality.

She will live with her Thea Pauline and Theo Jimmy and work in the White Star until she can start a sewing business and/or marry. She is grateful and excited. Her mind begins to spin with lists of all the things she must do to prepare. When the harvest is over and her plans are set, twenty-two year old Kiki makes a brief stop in a small town near Athens where a family friend helps her apply for her travel papers, costing 300 Drachma ($2,800 in current U.S. dollars). While she waits, she uses her Thea's additional funds to purchase a black mohair coat, a turquoise blue mohair dress with a flower embellishment and a pair of sturdy shoes. The rest of her belongings are left behind for her sisters. She purchases dress patterns for the latest fashion trends before boarding her ship the *Queen Fredericka* bound for the United States ten days later.

When she arrives in New York harbor, there is so much snow, all passengers are forced to stay aboard ship for an extra day. Fog and cold the following morning prevent the ship from coming into port, so small groups of passengers are eventually ferried to the dock in row boats. Kiki is met by Pauline's cousin and New York City resident Christina Alex, the picture bride who came to America from a small village near Lafka twenty-six-years earlier. Christina thoughtfully brings Kiki heavy boots, scarves, mittens and a warm coat for the long walk back to her home through knee deep snow. Kiki spends the next several snow-bound days getting a crash course on life in America.

When the weather finally improves, Christina puts Kiki on a train to Toledo. Tina and Ulysseus pick her up at the station and take her to see Pauline and Jimmy at the White Star. For the next several months, Kiki lives with her Theo and Thea and visits with her married cousins Angie, Joanne and Tina at Sunday dinners, or at their respective homes nearby.

"I missed my family in Greece," recalls Kiki Spounias, "but I was part of a loving new family with my Thea Pauline, Theo Jimmy and cousins. "It was like another world, but such a lovely world! I ate waffles and chocolate chip cookies for the first time at Joanne's apartment. My God! They were so good! Angie, Joanne and Tina would say, 'Kiki, you like everything!', and I really did! Especially vacuuming, because I had never seen a machine like that before. Thea Pauline used to joke that I would make her carpets threadbare, because I vacuumed them so often!"

"There were so many 'firsts': learning to use the telephone and flying with Angie's husband Dick to see The White Star and everyone's homes from the sky. These things were fantastical for someone like me!"

Shortly after her arrival, Tina and Ulysseus send a letter to Ulysseus' second cousin Chris Spounias, also recently immigrated to the U.S., to arrange a marriage. Kiki's first meeting with her prospective husband is over breakfast at the White Star. They discover they know several of the same people from neighboring villages in their *old country*. Chris extends an offer of marriage then stays four days at Tina and Ulysseus' house waiting for Kiki to say 'yes'.

"I remember going to Angie and Dick's house while we made wedding preparations," reminisces Kiki. "Their house seemed so huge to me. Chris started to get a little too friendly, so I said 'No! Not until we are married!' She says, able to laugh about it decades later. "Then, Thea Pauline drove us to Danville, Illinois, so I could meet his parents. They said Thea and Theo would have to pay for our wedding because I didn't have a dowry," Kiki recalls with disgust. "They didn't offer to pay for anything!"

Kiki and Chris eventually marry in a simple home ceremony with a Justice of the Peace. The bride wears Tina's wedding dress and her cousins don bridesmaid dresses from Joanne and John's recent wedding to stand up for her. After the brief ceremony, Pauline and Jimmy host a small dinner party for the wedding guests at their home on Haverfield Court.

Kiki's husband Chris becomes a dental technician and the two move to San Diego. With what little money they are able to save, Chris purchases run down rental properties and fixes them up in his spare time. Before long, they welcome a daughter Kostandena (Deanna) and fraternal twins Dimitra (Tammy) and Christos (Christopher). With the income from their rental properties, Kiki and Chris are able to bring Kiki's mother (Pauline's sister) Dimetra and Kiki's sisters Deanna and Soula over from Greece in 1977 and 1978 respectively. But over the years, Kiki's husband proves to be less than upstanding. He secretly borrows $15,000 from Pauline and Jimmy without Kiki's knowledge *"to pay off gambling debts"*, he tells them. But instead of paying off his debts, he purchases a gold Lincoln Continental.

"I was devastated when I found out," relates Kiki. "I said to him, 'How could you do that to my Thea Pauline after everything she has done for us?'"

Chris' solution is to take out a $100,000 loan secured by the values of their home and rental properties. He repays Pauline and uses the balance to purchase a piece of land on which to build three brand new rental properties. He also buys property in the mountains. These investments might have paid off handsomely over time if a balloon payment on his loan had not come due three years later.

When Chris can't make the steep repayment, the bank forecloses on *everything*, including their home. The family is forced to move into a small apartment. To salvage their finances, Kiki begins taking in sewing, but greater heartbreak lies ahead. A short time later, Chris secretly sells whatever remaining collateral he owns and flees to Greece, abandoning his wife and their three young children.

Fortunately, Kiki is used to hard work. She pulls herself up by the bootstraps and rents a closet-sized space in a friend's drycleaning shop to start her own seamstress business. She raises her family on a meager budget. With hard work and fortitude, Kiki grows her sewing business and rights her family's finances. Her oldest daughter Deanna becomes a pharmacist. Son Chris opens his own recreational tour business and his twin sister Tami eventually takes over the management of their mother's successful sewing business.

Changes

Back in Toledo, Ohio in 1967, construction of the Interstate highway expansion claims the land beneath the White Star Cafe, Jimmy and Pauline's nearby home and their small rental property. They receive a pittance of compensation through Eminent Domain and watch as the wrecking ball razes the repositories of their life's work over the last three decades. And just like that, at ages 72 and 56 respectively, Jimmy and Pauline are abruptly transitioned into retirement. It is a busy year, a shell game of moves and houses, not only for Pauline and Jimmy but also for two of their daughters. Dick, Angie and their two girls begin building a new home an hour from Toledo in the small town of Bryan, Ohio, adjacent to Dick's newly relocated plastics factory. John, Joanne and their three children relocate five hours away in Chicago where John accepts a new sales position. The timing of their move is perfect, allowing Jimmy and Pauline to buy the modest three bedroom they leave behind and begin making it their own.

When Dick and Angie's Toledo home sells before the construction on their new home is complete, the family temporarily moves into the offices of Dick's nearby factory, sleeping on cots, cooking in an electric skillet and washing dishes in the bathroom sink. Carol (9) and Karen (7) think it a grand adventure, turning factory handcarts into make-believe vehicles, building forts in the rafters of the stockroom and swan diving into piles of packing material from towering bails of flattened cardboard boxes. The same year, Dick earns a spot representing the United States in an international soaring competition in Argentina for the entire month of July. Children are not allowed, so Pauline and Jimmy take their two granddaughter Carol and Karen on a three month trip to Greece; ten weeks under Pauline's care while Dick and Angie. travel to Argentina and finish the construction on their home, and two additional weeks for Angie and Dick to join them in Greece for some sightseeing.

Jimmy, Pauline, Carol and Karen stay with Tasia Barges's family in Zevgolatio, arriving in 1968 during the final stages of construction of a second-story addition on their Greek home that includes indoor plumbing and running water for the first time. Carol and Karen marvel over things they have never seen before: the installation of terrazzo floors, the delivery of large blocks of ice to cool the wooden "ice box" and in place of a car, the family's open air wagon pulled by the same kerosine-powered tractor used to plow the family's fields. Many other things remain unchanged since Pauline's visit in 1957. Until the new construction is completed, the bathroom is still in an out building without electricity or running water. Showers are taken under the spigot of a suspended watering can. Clothes are still washed outside in a stone basin, and food continues to be baked in copper pots in the outdoor, wood burning, oven, promising mouth-watering meals of hand-picked produce seasoned with onions, garlic, oregano, mint and cinnamon... all infused with the aroma of wood smoke.

Karen (left) and Carol on the Barges Family's only powered mode of transportation.

The two girls make fast friends with the village children by staging daily treasure hunts for individually wrapped pieces of Bazooka Bubble Gum sent by the box full by their parents. Carol and Karen are fascinated by the mound of grain stored on the cool ground floor of their (Great Aunt) *Thea* Tasia's home, the wooden barrels of ground flour in the hall and the inherent maggots that are casually sifted out before each use. Yet, they have never tasted food so fresh or delicious, not to mention the daily walks to the bakery each morning to buy crusty rounds of warm bread.

Thea Tasia treats the girls to American style French fries with a Greek twist, frying them in freshly pressed olive oil. They are introduced to *Βανίλια* (A dollop of soft vanilla taffy served on a spoon in a glass of water, a refreshment typically offered to company), *vichenou* (cherries in a heavy syrup made of sugar and honey) and *lukumathes* (dollops of fermented doughnut-like batter fried in olive oil and sprinkled with cinnamon sugar or honey). And of course there are the amazing Greek pastries: *baklava* (chopped nuts mixed with cinnamon sugar sprinkled between layers of paper-thin *filo* dough brushed with butter that are rolled, baked, cut and drizzled with honey), *koulourakia (*twisted butter cookies), *Paximathia* (crunchy, anise flavored biscotti), *Kourabiethes* (short butter cookies with nuts buried under a dusting of powdered sugar) and magnificent *Dipples* (thin strips of flat noodle-like dough, swirled and fried in oil into blistered rosettes that are drizzled with honey and sprinkled with cinnamon and finely chopped walnuts). Heaven on earth!

Karen (left) and Carol Schreder by the out door oven.

Shyer, ten-year-old Carol spends most of her time in the house with the adults. Karen, two years younger, picks up enough Greek and sign language to disappear for much of the day with the local Greek kids, wrestling on rooftops, climbing the church's bell tower, daringly attending an electrocuted gypsy's funeral and sneaking off to feed bread to the neighbor's donkey. The girls get to know their heritage, their roots and their *YiaYia'* Pauline's side of the family. Pauline's mother Kostandina comes down from Lafka to spend time with them. Her great-granddaughters immediately notice her partially missing ring finger on her right hand.

"*YiaYia',* what happened to your finger?" They ask.

Pauline's mother Kostandina Athanasouli

She jokingly tells them that a *pontiki* (mouse) bit it off. But the girls later learn that her finger was snapped off when it got caught in the lead chain of a donkey she was walking down the mountain as a young girl. Trips to the ocean are made each weekend at top speeds of ten-miles-an-hour in the green metal wagon pulled by the family tractor. As the kids frolic in the warm Mediterranean water, the adults relax on the beach, piling sun-warmed rocks atop their arthritic joints. The Americans visit Xeni's house in the nearby village of *Braiebe* where Carol and Karen meet their second cousins, Xeni's grandchildren, Jenny (8) and Philipa (6). The four bond while wading in the cement drainage ditches and catching and swinging with the family's free range chickens. While it seems logical to Carol and Karen that their older relatives speak only Greek, they are puzzled by the communication issue with kids their own age.

"Come on," they say to Philipa and Jenny, convinced that they are playing tricks on them. "We know you guys can speak English." But of course they didn't.

Another memorable moment for the Americans is the emotional power a simple can of Campbell's Chicken Noodle Soup can pack. It is a surprise delivery by a distant Greek-American relative while he is in port on his U.S. Naval ship; a savory reminder of their American roots.

On weekends, the village of Zevgolatio comes to life with people enjoying grilled *Souvlaki* (lamb shish-ka-bobs), *Cafe'* (espresso), *Ouzo* (licorice flavored liquor) and *Bouzouki* music under strings of electric Edison light bulbs. There is a makeshift movie theater that shows American films with Greek subtitles, which Carol and Karen are midway through, when one of their playmates delivers the exciting news that their parents just arrived from America! The girls bolt from the theater, crying tears of joy at being able to see their parents after ten long weeks.

Over the next few days, they introduce their parents to all their new Greek friends and experiences. In return, they learn that the construction on their home back in Ohio is nearly complete. Dick, Angie, Carol, Karen, Jimmy and Pauline spend the final two weeks of their stay, exploring the cultural and historical treasures of Greece. They visit modern day Athens, the Acropolis, the Pantheon, the Treasury of Atreus and Delphi (Amphi) Theatre. The architectural accomplishments of their Greek ancestors have a profound impact on Carol and Karen who marvel at the beauty, sophistication and preservation of the ruins…as well as the noticeably short doorways.

They also visit their *Papou's* relatives in *Alea*, a poorer, more primitive village. Jimmy, Pauline, Carol and Karen stay overnight in the family's one-room, wooden home with a dirt floor. They are served a lavish meal by Alea standards of roasted chicken with the heads and feet still attached. And at night, the hosts graciously offer the Americans their own beds with sheets and blankets that are washed twice a year whether they need it or not; a real gut check for the coddled Americans.

~ ~ ~

Interestingly enough, the average person lives just long enough to experience the circle of life from a handful of distinctly different vantage points; as an innocent child, a parent, a grandparent, and if one is lucky enough, a great grandparent. Each iteration is witnessed and absorbed with greater maturity and insight that reframe life's experiences, entanglements and memories; much like the passage of time affects how historical figures are ultimately remembered.

During this trip, Pauline's life plays out for a third, bittersweet time. Her eight and ten-year old granddaughters are about the same age she was when she first left her mother and sisters for America. She witnesses how deeply Carol and Karen miss their parents and certainly must have wished anew that she could have been reunited with her mother and sisters after only a ten week separation.

After three full months visiting her family in Greece, it is once again time for tearful goodbyes. With each trip to her homeland, Pauline builds adult relationships with her mother and sisters on the foundations laid in her early childhood. But this time her sadness is tempered by promises that her sisters will visit her in America, and she will also return.

Life Back In America

When Jimmy and Pauline return to Toledo in 1968, they move into their daughter Joanne's former house. Like her first home on

Haverfield court, Pauline freshens the paint in each room, sews new curtains, spruces up the flower beds, plants a vegetable garden and maintains a picture perfect lawn. She even applies a fresh coat of metallic silver paint to the chain link fence, maintaining that, "More people see your home from the outside than the inside."

She helps out at her son-in-law Ulysseus and daughter Tina's Greek restaurant in downtown Toledo and partners with them to purchase, clean and manage a coin-operated laundromat.

In her free time, she quilts and embroiders bedspreads and pillow cases. She needlepoints and crochets miles of yarn into afghans, baby clothes, scarves, hats, purses and even starched snowflake Christmas tree ornaments. She sews beautiful prom dresses for her granddaughters on a treadle-driven sewing machine, working 'round the clock until she completes them to perfection. She expresses her love for her family through her actions: Sunday dinners, holiday gatherings, sleep overs, story telling, a trip to Greece, knitting and sewing, teaching them how to garden, taking them to the Greek Orthodox church and sharing the stories of past relatives during annual visits to the local cemetery.

Unfortunately, Jimmy's health begins to fail. He develops prostate cancer and suffers a series of debilitating strokes that render him unable to speak. Before long, he is unable to bathe, dress, shave or feed himself. He becomes bedridden and incontinent, requiring constant changing and the daily laundering of his clothes and bedding. It is exhausting work. And yet, Pauline insists on taking care of him at home and cooking holiday dinners to bring her daughters, sons-in-laws and grandchildren together.

For Greek Easter, she colors hard-boiled eggs and makes the traditional meal of roasted lamb and *Magyaritza soup* (Rich, homemade chicken broth with ground lamb, orzo pasta and lemon juice, thickened with frothy, beaten eggs). On New Year's Eve, she prepared a big meal followed by family card games of pinochle, poker and the much anticipated Greek tradition of cutting the loaf of bread with a silver dollar baked inside; the first piece cut for "the house" then each family member in succession by age from oldest to youngest. Having the knife *hit* the coin on *your* slice assures you of good fortune in the new year and is an exhilarating capstone to the celebration.

"FOOD IS SYMBOLIC OF LOVE WHEN
WORDS ARE INADEQUATE."
-ALAN D. WOLFELT

At one of these family gatherings, Pauline's son-in-law Ulysseus makes a comment that ruffles his sister-in-law Angie's feathers. He boasts that he is a self-made man, saying, "No one helped me when I came to America."

"Excuse me?" Angie interjects. "Who gave you a job when you first came to America…and a home in which to live rent free? Who helped you raise your son while you worked to build your restaurant? Who put money up to help you buy your laundromat and cleaned and managed it, sharing the profits 50-50? I'm not saying you're not a hard worker, but don't ever say 'no one helped you', because mom and dad did a lot for you."

In private, later that night, Pauline admonishes her oldest daughter, "You shouldn't have said that to Ulysseus, Angie. Didn't you feel me kicking you under the table? He'll never speak to you again."

But to Ulysses' great credit, he did.

A Funeral

In 1977, Angie makes arrangements for her father to temporarily stay in a nursing home in her home town of Bryan for two weeks, so her mother can travel to Greece to see her family and rest. Angie visits her father twice a day to feed him breakfast and dinner. Over the next two years, Jimmy makes two more brief stays in this nursing home, returning home to a more rested caregiver until his death on October 6, 1978. Jimmy's funeral service is held in Holy Trinity Greek Orthodox church in Toledo.

The ceremony begins with the traditional ringing of the church bell, calling mourners together as Jimmy's sons-in-laws and grandsons carry his casket into the church. His three daughters and wife follow behind. Pauline dresses in black from head to toe as her mother Kostandina did when her husband Thanasi died in 1957. Pauline is heartened by the sight of former patrons of the White Star and Club Cafe who come to pay their respects. Her heart catches when she sees Esther, Zina and Angie Athan from Newark too.

Her thoughts tumble through bittersweet memories as she listens to the hymns and prayers: meeting Jimmy for the first time, their wedding day, the success of The Club Cafe, Jimmy's practical jokes, walking away from The Club Cafe, opening The White Star, their joy at the birth of each of their daughters, the extravagant mouton fur coat and hat, Jimmy's alcoholism, finding him in the restaurant on Christmas Eve, his disappearances, his strokes, their struggles…and her absence from her own father's funeral. She feels a deep yearning for the comfort of her mother and sisters, dabbing tears from the corners of her eyes with one of her cherished childhood handkerchiefs that she embroidered with Mrs. White.

When the priest concludes the ceremony, Pauline's family and the congregation pay their final respects at the casket, genuflecting, kissing Jimmy's forehead, his hands or the nearby Greek religious icon, crossing themselves, lighting a candle and leaving remembrances of flowers. The priest then anoints Jimmy's body with oil and dust and closes the casket while reciting verses from the Old Testament in Greek.

At the cemetery, there is a brief *Trisagion*, or abridged funeral service. Family and friends stay to witness the lowering of his casket and the tossing of soil and flowers into the grave. Then the entire funeral party returns to the church for a *makaria*, or mourning luncheon of fish, which is an ancient Christian symbol and a traditional Greek meal during periods of sorrow. No desserts or sweets are permitted. Close friends and family continue to call on the family at their home where Angie, Joanne and Tina serve their guests wine, brandy, coffee and *Paximathia* (Greek biscotti).

FOOD IS THE MOST PRIMITIVE FORM OF COMFORT.
- SHEILAH GRAHAM

An official mourning period of 40 days follows, based on the time between Christ's crucifixion and his resurrection. During this period, Pauline and her family abstain from socializing. On the 40 day memorial service at the Greek church, the family prepares a large platter of *Koliva* (boiled wheat mixed with parsley, nuts, pomegranate seeds and sugar) to pass out in small bags to everyone in attendance. The *Kolvia* represents the natural cycle of seeds dying, being buried and rising again as new life, symbolically marking the release of Jimmy's soul from his physical body. These Greek traditions provide structure and comfort during the difficult processing of loss and grief. And before long, in the solitude that follows, Pauline once again feels the gravitational pull of her family from across the ocean.

Parsed Words

Twelve years have passed since her last visit to Greece. Pauline has stayed in touch through the exchange of wedding invitations, Christmas cards, photographs and brief phone calls at Christmas and Easter as the Pazos/Athanasouli families gathered together on separate continents. Although the cost of these calls drops dramatically over the years, the frugal parsing of words on both sides is a habit that is difficult to break. A typical conversation…

"Hello, Tasia! It's Panagiota! How are you?"

"Panagiota?!" Tasia says with surprise. Even though the phone call is anticipated, it always registers as a shock…and extravagance.

"Yes!"

Tasia places her hand over the receiver as she shares the exciting news with her house full of family. "It's Panagiota!" She says excitedly. Then back into the receiver, "Where are you?!"

"I'm in Toledo."

"She is calling from America!" Tasia says again over the mouthpiece to her family, then, "How are you, Panagiota?" As tears well.

"I'm fine," Pauline says as a broad smile lights her face and she wipes her eyes with a dinner napkin…as most calls are made over the remnants of a holiday meal. "How are you, Tasia?"

"Good."

"How is *Mama*?"

"Fine."

"Xeni?"

"Fine. Everyone is good. What do you hear from Dimetra in California?"

A condensed exchange of important updates from both continents follows, with each side using as few words as possible… to minimize the cost of the trans-Atlantic call.

From America…

"Dimetra says "hello". Angie and Dick's business is doing well. Joanne and John are healthy and doing well in Chicago. Business at Tina and Ulysseus's restaurant is steady. Their son Pano is going to school to become a doctor! Most of the other grandchildren are out of school and working."

From Greece…

"Our crops are good this year. Taki purchased his own bus and is driving between the villages and Athens at night. Chrísa is working for a bank, and Taki's son John is a security guard for a politician in Athens. Business at Xeni and Philipa's gas station is good."

And ends just as concisely…

"Okay, Tasia. I'll call you again at Easter. Merry Christmas!"

Bye, bye."

"Bye, bye! Merry Christmas, Panagiota!"

Details that cannot be gleaned by eavesdropping family members are enthusiastically shared and analyzed around the dinner table for the next hour. For Pauline, each call is like the thrill of finding a good book that keeps its reader charging through the pages toward a delicious ending, only to leave the reader craving more.

A Transformative Trip Home

In the summer of 1979, nine months after Jimmy's passing, Pauline returns to Greece for a third time; her first as a widow.

"I am going to stay until I get my fill of my mother!" She declares.

Once there, she and her mother share a joyful, tear-filled embrace; the mutual blackness of their clothing, blurring them into a single dark mass. But this time there is also a lightness; a new found ease. Over the years, they have managed to build a meaningful relationship that slips easily and comfortably over their shoulders, like a cherished, well-worn garment. They are relaxed in each other's company with a newfound sense of peace.

Pauline's mother, now 102 years old, is slowed, but still mobile and mentally sharp. She is the resilient mother of four living daughters, two in America (Pauline and Dimetra) and two still living in Greece (Xeni and Tasia) and three children buried long ago in the family crypt in *Lafka*, her infant son Spiro and two young daughters Olga and Eleni. She continues to live with her oldest daughter Xeni in the village of *Braibi*. From the proceeds of their modest gas station, they are able to add a small grocery store and build a second story onto their home with indoor plumbing to better serve the three generations living under the roof. Kostandina helps with light household tasks and keeps an eye on her great grandchildren while Xeni and Philipa manage the family businesses.

Pauline once again stays with Tasia, the sister she feels closest to, in *Zevgolatio*. When Tasia's husband Georgio dies, their oldest son Taki and his new wife Sophoula move in and take over, per Greek tradition. They have two sons *Georgios* (George) and *Yiani* (John). The three generations support themselves, harvesting apricots and almonds, growing table grapes and sun dried raisins and with Taki's earnings from his bus route.

A week into Pauline's visit, Xeni and Philipa make an unexpected appearance, telling Tasia and Pauline that their mother Kostandina is in pain, and they are driving her to the nearby hospital to see a doctor.

Tasia and Pauline race outside. They see their mother in obvious discomfort, sitting in an upholstered chair in the bed of Philipa's truck. She tells them she tripped over some toys in the middle of the night and fell on her hip. She waves off their concerns, assuring them she will be fine. But the doctors deliver bad news. Kostandina's hip is broken. In accordance with the Ancient Greek philosophy of stoicism, there is little intervention or treatment rendered, especially for patients of Kostandina's age. They simply advise Xeni and Philipa to *"Take Kostandia home and make her as comfortable as possible."*

STOICISM
A GREEK PHILOSOPHY THAT PAIN AND SUFFERING ARE NORMAL LIFE EVENTS THAT SHOULD BE ENDURED WITH LITTLE OR NO EMOTION.

For the next three weeks, Kostandina is confined to her bed in Xeni's home, and Pauline cares for her 'round the clock. She sits by her mother's bedside by day and sleeps on a pallet on the floor next to her bed by night. Her mother is most comfortable when lying flat on her back. But in the complete absence of pain medication, any movement for bathing, changing clothing or bed linens is an excruciating exercise. For Pauline, it is physically demanding work, But it allows her to convey her deeply felt, but rarely expressed love. And in return, Kostandina is able to lay down her own yolk of guilt. The two talk intimately, tearfully and at times, comically. It is a transformative period in both of their lives. After three difficult weeks, and despite Pauline's best efforts to nurse her mother back to health, Kostandina succumbs to complications from her injury; likely a combination of blood clots and pneumonia. She passes in the presence of three remaining daughters Xeni, Pauline and Tasia. Pauline later describes her mother's death and the events that followed as "The most amazing experience of [her] life."

Preparing The Body

The ringing of the early morning church bells confirm the news of Kostandina's death to the village. The reverberations dissipate the family's fog of disbelief, simultaneously fixing everything in reality and extinguishing any further hope for a miraculous recovery. It is a devastating loss for Pauline, that stands in jarring contrast to the calm acceptance and matter of fact actions of her sisters, who view their mother's death as a normal phase of life. There is much to do.

Xeni and Tasia teach Pauline the traditional ways of preparing their mother's body for her wake and burial. They reverently remove her clothing and place rolled strips of cotton cloth in her rectum to hold her bowels in place. Her long gray hair is washed, combed out and left to dry. They bathe her body with wine to retard the growth of bacteria and dress her in a clean set of the widow's clothing she has worn for nearly 30 years: black stockings, black shoes, a black skirt and blouse. Her hair, now dry, is combed, carefully wound into her signature bun and pinned at the nape of her neck. Next, a long strip of cloth is gently placed under her chin and tied at the top of her head to close her lax jaw. They place her body in a simple, tapered, wooden coffin, cover her body up to her chin with a white shroud and place her in the home's front room for 24 hours to allow her family and fellow villagers to pay their respects. Pauline and her sisters take turns sitting by their mother's body around the clock, so she is never alone. Each visitor brings a white flower, placing it on Kostandina's body until she is covered from toe to chin, except for a cross-shaped area on her chest which is filled in with red carnations from family members.

On the morning of the second day, the church bells ring again as her coffin is closed, loaded into a hearse with large viewing windows outlined with strings of miniature lights, and slowly driven up the mountain to *Lafka,* the village of her birth. Family members follow behind in Taki's bus. Word of Kostandina's death races ahead of the procession like the bow wave of a ship moving through water. And as they pass each village along the way, church bells reverberate, and people come out of their homes and shops to pay their respects.

On the outskirts of *Lafka,* the dirt road becomes increasingly rutted, forcing the family members to abandon the bus and finish the journey on foot behind the slow moving hearse. As they round the last copse of cyprus and olive trees that border the cemetery, the entire village…where Kostandia grew up, where she lived, worked and raised her family…once again forms a welcoming gauntlet on both sides of the road, standing solemnly and protectively this time to bear witness to the 360 degree completion of her life. As the hearse passes, many join the family's procession, first to the church for the funeral service, then to the cemetery.

The family's above ground crypt, Kostandina's final resting place, has been prepared. The bones of previous relatives have been taken to the church, blessed and placed toward the back of the grave to make room for Kostandina's wooden coffin. There is a small ceremony by the local priest. Incense is burned, her body is interred and the protective marble slab is somberly slid back in place. Before Pauline and her sisters leave, they place an oil-burning lamp and a cherished picture of Kostandina on the glass-enclosed shelf in the marble headstone.

It is a moment that resonates with perfect clarity for Pauline, as each end of their mother's lifeline snapped together.

Click!

Does anyone else hear it? Pauline's eyes dart to her sisters to see, but they are busy saying final prayers. And then, a profound feeling of peacefulness settles over her...a feeling of comfort, safety and "rightness". Her mother is *home*. She is at rest. Perhaps it is, as the Greeks believe, because her soul has reached its nebulous moment of release into the heavens.

She whispers *"P-a-n-a-g-i-o-t-a, M-a-m-a h-a-s d-i-e-d,"* to both her adult self and her nine-year-old alter ego, pulling the unimaginable words tightly around her like a protective cloak. *Twenty devastating letters...* And in the finality and acceptance of her mother's death, Panagiota, the child, and Pauline the woman, coalesce into a single, stronger version of their cleaved selves.

C H A P T E R 8

VISITORS

Back in the US in the years that follow, Pauline asks Angie for piece work from Dick's plastics factory to help put aside money for airline tickets for her sisters Tasia (Greece), Dimetra (California) and cousin Christina (New York City) to visit her on multiple occasions. She applies black ink to the perimeter of plastic protractors to darken the engraved radius numbers and markings, then wipes the excess ink off using paper towels. She does this in her home in shipments of 100's, 1,000's, 10,000's.

Over the next two decades, as her sisters also become widows, Pauline makes it possible for them to visit her in her snug, three-bedroom home; first Tasia. She stays for three months and is an uplifting houseguest. They speak Greek, laugh, crochet and visit the homes of Pauline's children and adult grandchildren. It is the first time Tasia has lived independent of her own extended family members; free of caring for others and able to fill her days as she and Pauline please. She later confides to her sister that she prefers this American way of living.

Soon Dimetra visits from California where she now lives with her daughters Kiki (whom Pauline and Jimmy helped bring to America in 1959), Soula and Dina. She stays with Pauline for two months, but life's hardships have darkened Dimetra's disposition, and it is a relief when it is time for her to return to California.

Her widowed cousin Christina Alex, the picture bride from New York City, is another regular visitor. Despite her husband's misrepresentations and chronic philandering, she never allowed her misfortunes to diminish the abundant wind in her sails. Her quick wit and sense of humor bring out the best in Pauline. The two joke, giggle and get into the kind of mischief that only two 88 year old women can, dancing at family weddings, telling funny stories and shouting Wendy's Old Fashioned Hamburgers' infamous 1980's marketing slogan *"Where's the Beef?"* with strong Greek accents. The two even join Angie and Dick on a cross country car trip to the American West where their schoolgirl antics continue.

During one of their private moments on this trip, the two make a pact that neither will attend the other's funeral. "We want to remember each other as beautiful women, like we are now...," Christina jokes in a thick Greek accent as she pats her hair and accentuates her not-so-hourglass figure. "...not when we're dead and ugly in a box!" Mugging a somber dead face. The two nudge each other and break into another fit of laughter.

The only sister who remains noticeably absent is Xeni.

More Changes

In 1986, Ulysses, Pauline's youngest daughter's husband, is diagnosed with bone cancer. Doctors in the United States do all they can for him to no avail. As a last ditch effort, he returns to Greece to try an experimental treatment which also proves ineffective. Tina joins him in Greece at Christmas in 1988, and he passes shortly thereafter. It is a blessing. Ulysseus had wanted to be buried in his Greek village, so his son Pano joins his mother in Greece for his funeral. He has visited his Greek relatives several times over the years, and yet, he experiences the same awe and solace at his father's funeral that Pauline experienced from her mother's nine years earlier.

When Tina and her son return to the US, she sells Ulysseus' restaurant and opens a smaller, more manageable fast food restaurant called The Wonder Dog. To supplement her income, she also does piece work for the Airmate Company. Five years later, she sells The Wonder Dog and begins commuting 60 miles to Bryan to work full time at Airmate. She stays with Angie and Dick during the week and returns to Toledo on the weekends.

"Why don't you just move to Bryan?" Angie asks her sister after a year of commuting.

"Oh, I could never leave Mother behind in Toledo," she replies.

"I'll bet mother would move to Bryan if you asked her," suggests Angie.

And so, in 1995, Tina and Pauline sell their respective homes in Toledo and build two modest new homes across the street from one another in the small town of Bryan, Ohio, a short drive from the Airmate Company. These are the first new homes for each. Pauline enlists the help of her daughter Joanne, the interior decorator in Chicago, who helps her mother coordinate carpet, cabinet styles, wall colors, light fixtures and wallpaper to go with her existing furniture. Pauline is thrilled with her lovely new home. But one month later, heavy rains overflow the surrounding drainage ditches, causing her single story home to flood with three inches of water; enough to ruin the brand new carpeting, drywall, paint and some of her furniture. She is devastated. Because it is an act of God, her insurance will not cover the damage, but Angie keeps that information from her mother and quietly pays for the repairs. The flood waters rise to the thresholds of Tina's house, across the street, but thankfully, never breached her home. When the water recedes, the County dredges the drainage ditches to eliminate future flooding, but Pauline remains vigilant during even the slightest rain shower.

With the repairs complete, Pauline once again welcomes her sister Tasia to her new home for extended stays. But her cousin and sidekick Christina Alex doesn't return. True to their pact, when Pauline receives the news of Christina's death, she sends flowers and her condolences, but she does not travel to New York for her funeral.

Happy occasions are a different story for Pauline. Over the next several years, She attends the graduations and weddings of her six grandchildren and rejoices in the birth of each of her fourteen great grandchildren. To say she loves babies is an understatement. They are her little paper dolls. She dresses, changes and talks lovingly and unabashedly to them. The mother-child relationship remains sacred to Pauline. She visits her granddaughter Karen after the birth of her first set of twins and marvels at the miracle of having two babies to cuddle at one time. The nursed twins develop rolls of fat like cherubs.

"That Karen!" Pauline exclaims. "She must have milk like whipping cream! Maybe she can keep one and give the other one to me," she suggests half-jokingly, remembering an actual precedent for this within her extended family that settled in Hollywood, California. Angie's Godmother Chrisanthy Economu was unable to have children. When her sister became pregnant for the second time, Chrisanthy predicted she was going to have twins and asked if she would give her one of them." Her sister did indeed have twin boys, and as promised, gave one to her sister. The sisters' two families lived next to each other and raised all three children together.

Opinions

In stark contrast to her quiet, observing childhood, Pauline becomes more outspoken and direct in her later years, but never from a mean-spirited place. Upon seeing her middle-aged grandson George Copetas for the first time in quite awhile, she hugs him tightly before holding him at arm's length and declaring, *"George, you're losing your hair!"*

As Angie moves into her seventies, Pauline interrupts one of their casual conversations to inform her, "You have a lot of chin hairs, Angie."

"Well," Angie replies, good naturedly, "I guess I'll never have to worry about becoming unkempt as I age, because I'll have my mother to tell me!"

When a family friend visits the Pazos clan, sporting a new and not so flattering mustache, Pauline sits quietly in the corner, thumb under her chin with her forefinger covertly see-sawing back and forth across her upper lip, as if to say "Look at that awful mustache!" A mischievous antic of which her comedic cousin Christina would have been proud!

For granddaughter Karen, Pauline always provides a soft place to land. She stays with her *YiaYia'* on numerous summer weekends, running through her sprinklers, building forts in the rafters of her garage as a child, and in her teenage years, arriving with patterns and fabrics for her *YiaYia'* to sew beautiful prom dresses. As she grows into an adult, the two share similar interests: cooking, gardening and traditional home decor.

Pauline admires the thoughtfulness of Karen's husband Randy… "He's a real gentleman!"…as well as the good looks of Randy's silver-haired father about whom she frequently observes with heavily rolled "r's, "That Mr. Barbera is a very handsome man!"

Shortie

In 2002, Angie and Pauline travel to Tucson, Arizona to visit Karen in her new desert home where decorating and gardening are completely different from those in the Midwest. Always observant and curious, Pauline investigates everything in great detail. She is particularly enthralled by the outdoor lifestyle and desert cacti and succulents. Ever the green thumb, she snaps off a few cuttings to smuggle home and root.

The three generations of women vary in height like descending stepping stones. When they venture out for an alfresco lunch one afternoon, they run into one of Karen's business acquaintances. She proudly introduces her mother and grandmother, adding the humorous qualifier, "And we get progressively shorter as we age!" Before long, *"Shortie"* becomes Karen's pet name for her *YiaYia*, which always elicits a hearty laugh from both.

The Importance of Home

Home means a lot to Pauline. It signifies family, love, safety and speaks of one's work ethic and sense of style. There is an unspoken expectation from Pauline that if you do nothing else, you will take pristine care of your home, inside and out. Pauline's own housekeeping sets a high standard. Despite limited budgets, her homes are always orderly, stylish and welcoming. Everything has an appropriate place, and items that outlive their usefulness are either sent to Greece or donated to those in need. Her bedroom closet holds only a handful of housecoats, a dress or two, a few pairs of shoes and slippers. She is sentimental and loyal to people throughout her life, but never to possessions. Even her wedding dress falls victim to her relentless decluttering.

Her only personal indulgences? Birds, plants, her daily TV soap operas and dolls. She keeps a succession of yellow canaries, all named Lucky, in a tidy bird cage in the corner of her kitchen. They give her something to nurture. She keeps their cage stocked with water, seeds, fresh lettuce leaves, and on occasion, a nibble of sugar from her finger. On her window sills are perpetual pinches of new plants rooting in glasses of water next to pots of delicate African violets, baby-tear, philodendron and a variety of thriving potted plants throughout her house. She is a master of growing, fertilizing, trimming and repotting. If you have an ailing plant, you take it to Dr. Pauline, and in short order, she returns a lush, botanical specimen. She is a bottomless pit of nurturing, caring and doing.

She is also fascinated by her daily soap opera, which gives her an acceptable excuse to slow her hummingbird pace, set up her TV-tray and fix herself...or any visiting family member...a tasty lunch; usually accompanied by a handful of Ruffles potato chips and a Flintstone jelly-jar glass of Pepsi Cola poured over dense chunks of ice cracked from her metal, louvered ice trays.

And then there is her love of dolls. "When I was a little girl," recalls her granddaughter Karen, "she asked me to give her my favorite dolls for a week. I had a life-sized 'walking' doll, a "Chrissy Doll" and a small babydoll that I hated to part with, but she assured me she would take good care of them and return them with "a surprise".

True to her word, Pauline returns the dolls dressed in new, hand sewn, perfectly-fitted outfits: dresses, coats, hats, even underwear and slips. What a wonderful surprise!

"I spent hours dressing them up and down," recalls Karen, "but it wasn't until I got older that I appreciated the significance of her gift. I realized that dolls, like the paper dolls she cut out as a young girl with Mrs. White in her apartment above the millinery shop, were especially comforting to her. She took care of them like she wished she could have been taken care of by her own mother. And they became a medium through which she could openly express her love and emotions."

"When my mother was in her 80's, I took her to an art festival," recalls Angie. "She fell in love with a baby doll that was so incredibly life-like, you could mistake it for a real baby. She had a hard time putting it down, but she couldn't bring herself to pay what she felt was an extravagant price. My one regret to this day is that I didn't buy the baby doll for her and surprise her with it as a gift."

After years of cooking at the White Star, Pauline becomes an accomplished cook who makes feeding a crowd on a moment's notice look effortless. There is always a beautifully set table filled with beef or lamb roasts, baked chicken, manestra, home-made mashed potatoes with gravy, roasted vegetables, salads, home-made Greek yogurt and fresh-baked bread. She knows each person's favorite treat and becomes a virtual pastry chef, turning out apple, rhubarb, berry, pecan, lemon meringue and coconut cream pies, cakes, puddings, and of course her signature Greek desserts: *baklava, koulourakia, pakshimathakia, kourabiethes, dimples* and *melomakarona.* With every visit, she arrives with a tin of baked goods, a hand-stitched, crocheted or embroidered gift or freshly potted plant.

New Neighbors

By 1997, Angie's husband Dick is diagnosed with early stages of Parkinson and Alzheimer Diseases. He takes a tumble down a full flight of carpeted stairs in their three-story home. Pauline, who happens to be visiting Angie at the time, expresses her amazement and relief.

"That Dick!" She exclaims when she realizes he is unhurt. "He's built like a brick!"

Angie senses the time has come to begin searching for a more accessible, single-story home. During this same time, Tina receives a job offer to work for a friend and jeweler based in New Orleans. It is a chance for her to spread her wings for the first time since her husband's death. The timing couldn't be better. In another round of *musical houses,* Dick and Angie offer to purchase Tina's ranch-style home. Its floor plan will be more accessible for Dick, Tina will be able to move to the Big Easy, and with its proximity to Pauline's house just across across the street, Angie will be able to look in on her mother.

~ ~ ~

Pauline walks over at Angie's house for dessert one evening. Angie offers her mother and her husband some angel food cake with strawberries and whipping cream. Dick, now in his early eighties, looks quizzically at his wife as he takes his plate from her and asks, "Where's Angie?"

Angie is taken aback, but recovers quickly. "Who do you think *I* am?" She asks.

"Well…," Dick says as he studies her blankly, "I guess you're Angie…but where is the *other* (younger) Angie?"

Instead of taking care of her mother, Angie becomes the caregiver for her eighty-year old husband for the next five years. Pauline, still sharp and mobile in her late 90's, helps by babysitting her son-in-law from time to time while Angie runs out for occasional meetings or groceries.

C H A P T E R   9

A FINAL HOMECOMING
2007

In August, 2002, Dick passes away. Pauline helps a second daughter bury her spouse. Over the next few years, Pauline begins to feel the physical effects of her age, but rarely complains. Still, her own declining health becomes apparent in her actions. She turns over the keys to her 1988 blue Chrysler LaSabre to her great grandson, Andrew Presnar, and relies on Angie to shuttle her to and from the grocery store, medical appointments and family gatherings.

At the age of 94, Pauline has cataract surgery. It restores her vision, but unfortunately, not her youthful strength. Her heart is inflamed, reducing her stamina, and the arthritis and calcification along her spinal column causes her discomfort when she is on her feet for extended periods. For the first time in her life, she hires someone to cut her grass, but still continues to water and weed the flower beds that encircle her home. She keeps her outdoor bird feeders brimming with seeds to attract the little birds she so dearly loves and hangs her laundry outside on the clothesline year 'round as she has done her entire life.

Over toast and coffee one morning, Pauline says to Angie, "I wish I could make one last trip to Greece to see Tasia."

"Well, why don't you?" Challenges Angie. "There is nothing stopping you."

Pauline hems and haws, throwing out chaff, "I don't know. It's a long trip. I'm old. The tickets are expensive now."

"You can afford to go, mom," says Angie, who has handled her mother's finances since the early days of the White Star. "…And, if you want, I'll go with you. I bet Karen will go too."

"You'll go? Karen Too?" Asks Pauline, perking up. Then more matter of fact, as if she is thinking about buying a "so-so" pair of shoes, "I'll think about it."

The next day, Pauline calls Angie, "I talked with Sophoulla (Tasia's daughter-in-law) on the phone today. She is expecting the three of us next month."

"What?" Asks Angie, thinking she didn't hear her mother correctly.

"I told Sophoula that we are all coming, but I told her not to tell Tasia about me…just you and Karen," says Pauline with a mischievous smile. "I want to surprise my sister!"

"Oh my gosh!" Exclaims Angie. "This will be fun!" Mother and daughter laugh together as they imagine Tasia's surprise. Angie adds to their merriment by telling her mother, "Your cousin Christina would be so proud of you!"

This will mark Pauline's sixth trip to Greece to visit her family over the last eight decades since she left as a nine-year-old in 1919:

1.) 1957…when she was 46 years old
2.) 1969…at age 58
3.) 1980…at age 69
4.) 1997…at age 86
5.) 2004…at 93 and…
6.) 2007…at age 96

It's a running joke among Pauline's American family that she has made at least two, self-declared *"last trips"* to Greece. But this time, with her inflamed and inefficient heart, Pauline knows with certainty that… *"T-h-i-s i-s m-y l-a-s-t t-r-i-p h-o-m-e."* Twenty painful letters.

Zevgolatio, Greece

Angie scurries to make their international travel arrangements, and by November 2007, their trip is arranged. She calls Greece and finalizes their arrival time into Athens. Sophoulla tells her that Angie's cousin Themo Bilianis and his wife Deanna will pick them up at the airport. She also assures Angie that Pauline's secret arrival is still intact. Tasia is eagerly awaiting only Angie and Karen.

In addition to her traditional gifts of linens and towels, Pauline packs a jumble of emotions: anticipation laced with foreboding, joy followed closely by the certainty of bereavement. Gone is the protective restraint that has served her so well over the years. She travels to Greece this time with an open and unguarded heart, to be filled one last time from the well of her family.

Pauline, Angie and Karen arrive safely in Athens and are picked up from the airport by Angie's cousin Themo and his wife Deanna. The jovial couple drive the three women 96 kms to Zevgolatio. Karen's first trip to Greece in 1968 as a seven-year-old and this trip in 2007, as a thirty nine-year-old somewhat parallel her *Yia'Yia's* departure from Greece as a nine-year-old and her first return trip as a forty-nine-year-old. And she experiences some of the same thoughts and emotions her *Yia-Yia* experienced upon her return to Greece in 1957, like walking into a time capsule of familiar sights, smells, childhood memories and disappointments. When they pull up in front of Tasia's home, Karen immediately notices the stone wash basin and the outdoor oven are no longer there, and the well has been leveled and covered with a heavy sheet of metal.

But Tasia's house looks the same! As the Americans ascend the steps to the front door, they are met with hugs, kisses and a burst of hushed Greek endearments from Sophoulla. Then, Sophoulla leads Pauline into the house where Tasia is waiting. The two sisters lock eyes; Pauline knowingly, Tasia with a look of confusion as she struggles to make sense of what her eyes are telling her. But hearts know what they know. Words become unnecessary. The two sisters embrace, mingling the tears on their cheeks. Their reunion, tugs at the hearts and blurs the vision of everyone present.

Oblivious to one another's gray hair, crinkly skin, widow's clothing and Pauline's cane, they welcome the young girls they once were…and the old women they are now…two sisters with similar faces, yet divergent life paths. They sit close to one another, holding hands to help savor and root their reunion in reality.

Sister Tasia (left) and Pauline share a tearful embrace

Karen is re-introduced to relatives she has not seen since her childhood trip. The adults are vaguely familiar, but the children have grown and changed beyond recognition. Angie does her best to translate the highlights of the swirling Greek dialogue. Karen gets to know Sophoulla, the wife of Tasia's oldest son Taki, who died of a sudden heart attack in his 40's, and their two grown sons Georgios (George) and Yiani (John). As the oldest son's wife, Sophoulla takes care of her mother-in-law in the same house Pauline, Angie and Karen stayed at in 1968. It is freshly painted with modern windows and appliances that Pauline has helped fund over the years, but Karen's later explorations thankfully reveal many things that have stayed the same: the layout of the house, the terrazzo flooring, the marble kitchen counter and the original, first-floor where the visiting Americans and the Barges family briefly lived until the construction of the home's second floor was completed. The first floor now serves as a storage area. Karen is warmed by the sight of her Thea Tasia's old copper cooking pots, hanging on the walls, touchstones that validate her memories.

Sophoulla and Tasia prepare a meal to welcome their new guests, and everyone gets reacquainted. Twenty-five-year-old Georgios, the eldest son, lives at home per Greek tradition. He invested in a new bus and continues to drive his father's route to support the family. Yiani, two years younger, keeps an apartment in Athens where he provides security for a government dignitary. During spring and summer months, Sophoulla and her boys still work the family's land, but the frenzy of the harvest is now over, and it is a perfect time to visit. Karen's childhood playmate pops over after dinner to say hello from the house next door where he still lives with his wife and three teenage daughters. Karen brushes a heavy layer of rust off of her rudimentary Greek and greets him with enthusiasm.

"Geia sas, Georgio! Einai kalo' koritsi."

There is a burst of laughter as her mother informs her that she has just told George *"Hello!"* And that he is *"...a very good girl!"* It establishes a humorous tone that sets the mood for the entire trip as the three generations of *Pazos/Athanasouli/Barges* women take a lengthy stroll down memory lane.

As it so happens, they have arrived during the local political elections, a stroke of luck. Zevgolatio is the seat of the Vocha municipality where local citizens are required to return once a year to vote. It creates an annual homecoming event. News of Pauline's visit spreads quickly, and a stream of people stop in to say hello. Sophoulla's home morphs into a life-sized Cuckoo Clock with the circular movements of well-wishers coming in through the front door with small gifts, laughing over shared memories and departing through the side door. With a limited understanding of Greek, Karen is left to puzzle the significance of each acquaintance through tidbits of translations, the length of the visit and the amount of laughter. One of her favorites comes from *Eirini*, one of her *YiaYia* Pauline's cousins who tells how she nearly killed her brother-in-law as a young newlywed...

"I was a new bride still getting familiar with my in-law's home when my brother-in-law came over for dinner," recalls *Eirini*. "I cooked a big meal, wanting to make a good impression. After dinner, my husband said to me, *'Eiríni*, bring our guest a shot of *Ouzo.'* So I went into the kitchen, got a nice tray out, poured a generous shot of *Ouzo* into a nice glass, put it on the tray and dutifully offered it to him."

"He smiled at me...(*Erini* smiles, pantomiming her brother-in-law's every move)... 'gave me a nod of thanks...(nods)...took the glass and swallowed the *Ouzo* in one quick gulp (throws her head back). Then, without saying a word, he placed the empty glass on the table…(*Erini* pats the table with her hand)…nodded his head to both of us…(nods twice)…, and walked straight out our front door… (gestures towards Tasia's front door)."

"We thought it was odd," continues *Erini*, starting to laugh, "but figured he must have had things to do." She begins to laugh harder, knowing what comes next. "Later, when I was cleaning up the kitchen, my husband said, '*Erini*, Why do you have the weed killer out?'"

"'The weed killer?' I asked, confused."

"'Yes,' my husband said as he pointing to my bottle of *Ouzo*, 'The weed killer.'"

"My eyes got as big as walnuts," confesses *Erini*, "because (laughing) I realized… (laughing harder) I just poisoned my brother-in-law!" (More laughter).

"WEED KILLER?!?" Someone howls over the group's hysterical laughter.

"OH MY GOD, *Eiríni*!" Someone else exclaims in the middle of more laughter and disbelief.

"So," chortles *Eiríni,* doing her best to continue her story as the group gets caught up in a laughing jag, "I said to my husband (laughing) in the calmest voice I could, 'Oh, no reason. (Laughing) I'll just put it away right now'."

"More like 'HIDE THE EVIDENCE!'" Someone exclaims, to even more laughter, while Angie tries her best to continue translating for her non-Greek-speaking daughter Karen.

"'He drank it," says *Erini* through deep belly laughs and tears, "and never said another WORD about it that day, or the entire time we were married!"

Then, trying for a more sober tone, "I can laugh now," she tries to explain, composing herself just long enough to gasp, "because he didn't die!"

Another explosion of laughter rocks the group.

"What did I know back then?!" Erini manages to squeak, rhetorically.

"NOT MUCH!" Quips Pauline with the timing of a seasoned stand-up comedian, causing everyone's laughter to liquify and roll down their cheeks.

Election Weekend

After the election weekend, life settles back into its normal rhythms. Tasia's daughter Chríssa and her husband Dino stop by for dinner. They were young, beautiful and newly married when Karen last saw them. "…like royalty back then," she recalls. As they visit with Angie, Karen joins her second cousin Sophoulla as she heads outside to meet a neighbor who is helping her brew her inaugural batch of wine. She is fermenting it in a blue, fifty-gallon plastic barrel under an awning in the side yard. As the two of them peer into the contents of the barrel, the neighbor confirms that the aroma and tiny bubbles from the wild airborne yeasts mean the fermentation process is well underway.

"Does it have enough sugar?" Sophoulla asks. "Is it time to strain it and remove the crushed grape skins?"

Her neighbor stirs the contents and tastes it before answering in the affirmative to both of Sophoulla's questions. She samples it as well and nods her agreement. Karen helps Sophoulla pull up the heavy cheesecloth lining the barrel, and with it, all of the unwanted solids. The remaining *"must"* will be left in the barrel a bit longer to age and soften the tannins before being more finely strained and served as the family's private table wine.

"It was such a straightforward approach," recalls Karen. "It reminded me that processes like wine making evolved organically over time in small batches through trial and error and with a little help from one's friends…the way it was meant to be. In the U.S., we tend to make everything so clinical and complicated that it loses the important connection to the land, the people who grew the grapes, the food it will be consumed with and each family or regions' unique tastes." When Sophoulla later serves some of the neighbor's wine with dinner, it is as good as any Karen has tasted.

In the late afternoons, while Pauline and Angie visit with Tasia and Sophoulla in the house, Karen ventures out to explore the village on foot, looking for familiar sights. She spots the church where she and the local boys snuck in to watch gypsy's funeral as well as several abandoned outdoor ovens and rusty tractors similar to the ones from her memories, but there is no trace of the ice cream shop, the lye pit or the neighbor's donkey she once befriended.

On the fourth day, Sophoulla, Pauline, Angie and Karen drive up the mountain to Pauline's childhood home in Lafka. Tasia is reluctant to accompany them because of the motion sickness she experiences riding in cars. To help minimize it, they buckle her into the front seat and crack her window for a steady stream of fresh air. The trip, which once took 11 hours by donkey, is completed in an hour and a half, and Tasia fares well. They stop at the cemetery at the outskirts of the village. There, they visit the family crypt where Pauline's mother, father and siblings are buried. They share family stories, burn incense and leave flowering plants as remembrances. This is a ritual that allows Pauline to pay her respects and savor her fondest memories; a reunion of sorts with stories to be shared, and laughed or cried over.

The five women continue up the mountain a few more miles and make a brief, but emotional stop at the home of Pauline's cousin Athanasios Athanasoulis, whose four brothers were slain by the German soldiers during World War II. Like Pauline, he is also in his late 90's.

Next, they head to Pauline's childhood home. What was once a one-room structure built on a stacked stone foundation, is now a lovely enlarged and renovated two-story, stone and stucco structure. Karen is introduced to the relatives living there and taken on a tour of the pristine home as her *Yia-Yia* fills in the historical detail. Pauline shakes out each piece of her family's history as if she is spring cleaning her memories and carefully passing them on to the next two generations.

Lafka is more reminiscent of the Zevgolatio village Karen visited 40 years earlier; still swaddled in the wonderful aromas of earthiness and wood smoke. She is excited when Sophoulla links arms with her and gestures for Karen to join her on a walk through Lafka as if to say, *"Let the old people talk while I show you the village."*

Stepping Back In Time

The two set off on foot. Karen is flattered by Sophoulla's attention, but it soon becomes clear that her relative has a secondary motive; a rental property with *a problem*. Sophoulla pulls Karen along on a collision course with a man suspected of mismanaging her old family home. She is shrewd enough to know the value of having a protective wingman, even if that person comprehends only a handful of Greek words. They eventually come to a stop in front of a noble-looking house with a jumble of furniture stacked outside. As Karen wonders why they have stopped at this particular house, Sophoulla jumps into a heated discussion with a Greek man who is converging on the property from the opposite direction.

*Hmmm…*Karen thinks. *This is an unexpected turn of events.* She puts on her best poker face, and takes a page out of her *YiaYia'* Pauline's book, receding into the background to quietly observe the events as they unfold: raised voices, flamboyant hand gestures, hostile body language and a smattering of Greek words that she recognizes…*Chairs. Beds. Outside. Yugoslavia. Ten. Big. Boys. Girls. American.*

"American? Oh God! What am I being dragged into?" She wonders, shifting her gaze between Sophoulla and the man. It doesn't take long to deduce that the man is the unpopular property manager…and she has been brought along for reassurance… backup. The volume and intensity of the two's discussion brings a number of neighbors out onto their balconies to chime in on the conversation with their own observations. They seem to be agreeing with Sophoulla and calling out the inaccuracies of the property manager's statements.

Is this normal? Wonders Karen as she looks for clues. *Do people just jump right into each other's business like this?*

If everyone's body language is any indication, the answer appears to be a resounding *"Yes!"* There are now three Greek (and one reluctant American) women standing up to an increasingly exasperated Greek man. As tensions escalate, Karen begins looking for exit routes and calculating the odds of outrunning a potential assault. She widens her stance and is encouraged by the fact that she is the tallest of the five by nearly a foot. But the altercation eventually simmers down then ends as quickly as it flared up. The man leaves with his tail tucked between his legs. The neighbors wave goodbye to Sophoulla and go back into their homes. But instead of beating a hasty retreat, Sophoulla steers Karen into the house, which was once her family home.

A tour? An inspection? Karen wonders, uncertain whether either is prudent after hearing the few cryptic words she understood. She is dragged through the front door and instantly transported back in time by more than a century. It is a handsome house with stone walls and classic proportions. There is no electricity, no bathroom and no furniture except for a number of beds and a couple of butane-powered hot plates scattered about. *Of course...* Karen puts two and two together...*all the other furniture is outside!* The dubious landlord has been renting the house out to 10-12 young Yugoslavian field workers without Sophoula's knowledge.

Karen is struck by the chiseled stone sink in the kitchen with a hand pump for water. The only heat is presumably generated by the large stone fireplace with a striking image of a Greek Warrior finely chiseled in its tapered stone hood. Karen snaps a few hasty photos as Sophoulla moves from one room to another, inspecting and muttering phrases of disapproval under her breath. When she is finally satisfied, she once again locks arms with her American compatriot and retraces their steps back through the village.

The language barrier minimizes further discussions, but Karen keeps her head on a precautionary swivel just in case. It is late afternoon when they rejoin Tasia, Pauline and Angie and time to leave if they hope to make it home before dark. They say their goodbyes and begin their drive back to Zevgolatio.

With access to her trusty translators once again, Karen begins a humorous dissection of her interpretation of Sophoulla's run-in with the *evil landlord.* Her story comes out in short bursts, so Angie and Pauline can stop laughing long enough to translate. It is now Sophoulla and Tasia's turn to say *"Neh! Neh!" (Yes! Yes!)* here and there and laugh as they affirm the accuracy of Karen's observations and offer additional humorous insights of her own. And the story continues as the five travel down the mountain, laughing until their faces and stomachs hurt. It is a bonding experience, and one of the best "girls' outings" in recent memory for all.

Gifts

It's funny how a small part of us earnestly and irrationally hopes for everything to remain unchanged when returning to familiar places of personal significance…as if we can temporarily revisit and catch glimpses of our same selves from an earlier period of our lives…to gain greater insights from a more mature perspective. The power of returning "home" to one's roots is undeniable. It comforts, enlightens, heals. It provides context between who we once *were* and who we currently *are*, and we emerge with greater insight into the elemental identities of our true selves and those around us.

If we slow down and take notice, we have the wonderful opportunity to experience any number and variety of *gifts* during our lifetimes. For Pauline, the latest is the timing of her final trip home during election week. It is an unexpected stroke of luck to see so many friends and relatives from her past in such a condensed and spontaneous fashion. It is like experiencing all the benefits of one's own wake first hand, under happier circumstances. Her entire trip is an organic, relaxed, mixture of family, friends, familiar places, stories, laughter and the unspoken changing of the guard.

There is little that can match the comfort that comes from having a long history with friends and loved ones; the privilege of witnessing the big and small moments in each others' lives, of being understood in the context of our actions and hopefully our lives well-lived; and if we are lucky, to reap the rare and resulting benefits: compassion, loyalty, trust, and the ability to nakedly be who we are without fear of judgment or rejection.

Pauline re-experiences her heritage through the fresh perspective of her daughter Angie and granddaughter Karen; another life lesson on the power and importance of family. It is so joyous, funny and energizing that it never occurs to Karen that it will likely be her final trip with her *YiaYia'* Pauline. How foolish we can often be, taking for granted that the people who have played integral roles in our lives will always be with us, that our time with them will be infinite. Perhaps it's our subconscious way of protecting our own hearts.

The Matriarch

The unwavering love for her family, quietly pulsing within Pauline, has bound her loved ones to her…and each other… across oceans, continents and time. She has been a fighter…a survivor.

She has endured, persevered and made do. She suppressed her own needs to invest in her family and lived her life with integrity, grit, hard work, hope, optimism and service to others.

She returns home conscious of her diminishing stamina. Angie takes her to the Emergency Room as a precaution later that same year when her breathing becomes labored. The doctors diagnose her with congestive heart failure and estimate that she has 4-6 months to live. Hospice is called, and Angie moves in with her mother to provide 'round the clock care and companionship. Pauline is still mobile and mentally sharp, but her body is weakening. Her spinal stenosis causes her discomfort. She endures persistent pain in her upper right shoulder. She tires easily when standing or walking. Her granddaughters rub her painful shoulder, her muscular hands and legs, but it provided little lasting relief. And in a rare moment of candor, Pauline confides to Karen, "I never thought I would get like this," referring to her lack of stamina and inability to "*do*".

In true Greek warrior fashion, Pauline proves her doctor's diagnosis wrong. A year passes. The family jokes that she graduated from Hospice at least 2-3 times. And always one to have things neat and tidy, she makes sure her family knows her final wishes; to be buried next to her husband Jimmy in the family plot in Toledo. She makes a trip to the local funeral home with her daughter Angie and granddaughter Carol to make preparations. Channeling her comedic cousin Christina, she walks through the showroom, leaning her head into a variety of open caskets, asking, "How do I look against this lining color?" Followed by bursts of her signature, high pitched laugh.

As the end nears, just two years short of her 100th birthday, Pauline finds herself at home in her bed surrounded by her three daughters, Angie, Joanne and Tina. Her mother, father and Jimmy have been speaking to her in her dreams for some time now. She longs to be with them again, but she is at war with herself. How does she suddenly *give up* when her entire life has been defined by fighting and persevering? Her daughters' final gift is their love, encouragement…and *permission* to stop fighting.

"We love you, mom. Everything is going to be okay. We'll be fine. It's time for you to be with your *mama* and *Baba*…and daddy. You'll see Christina, Uncle Brother Pete, Uncle Cousin

Pete, your sisters Xeni and Demitra…your baby sisters Olga and Eleni…and your baby brother Spiro. It's okay. We'll be fine…

"Y-o-u c-a-n g-o h-o-m-e n-o-w, M-a-m-m-a."

EPILOGUE

Panagiota (Athanasouli) Pazos would have enjoyed her funeral. She was always happiest surrounded by her family who were drawn together for the first time in many years. One of her Chicago grandsons Jimmy Copetas shares a humorous recollection in his eulogy.

"I was sitting in the dugout during one of my high school baseball games, when a teammate nudged me, pointed to the adjacent abandoned lot and asked rather incredulously, 'Hey Jim, isn't that your grandmother over in that field…pulling weeds?!'

"I looked over, and sure enough, there was my *Yia'Yia'*…on her hands and knees in her signature dress with her over-the-knee stockings and conservative, low-heeled pumps…pulling tender dandelion greens from the ground with a flathead screwdriver and plopping them in a neat pile atop a freshly spread newspaper."

"'Yep, that's her,' I replied nonchalantly, but with a sense of great pride, 'She's pulling dandelion greens…and we'll probably be eating them later tonight!'"

"Cooked Dandelion greens with a little lemon juice, olive oil, vinegar and salt was one of my *Yia'Yia''s* specialties," Jimmy continued. "My mouth is watering right now just talking about it!"

~ ~ ~

Sometimes, at the end of a busy day, I pour myself a fresh cup of coffee and walk around the exterior of my home at twilight, trying to see it and my life objectively as a stranger might. The words I heard my *Yia'Yia'* say so many times, resonate in my head, "Take care of your yard and the exterior of your home. More people see it from the outside than the inside." But she also taught us how to turn the *inside* of our houses into homes…with equal parts of paint, sewing, green plants, elbow grease, home cooking, and of course, lots of love. But above all, she taught us the importance of family.

I think of *Shortie*…when I see a little bird, when I cook a good meal, when I clean my home, when I see a baby, when I help my own daughters try on dresses for their high school dances, when the subject of immigrants comes up, when I see a nine-year-old girl, when I see my aunts and cousins, or when I see, hear or taste anything Greek.

For all the difficult and unfair things she experienced during her life, she never carried a grudge or became bitter, even when it came to her *Thea* Sophia. She didn't forget her mistreatment, but she chose to focus on the positive things she learned. When I go through tough times, I think of her inner strength, and know I can certainly persevere. I hope she is proud of us…of the lives we have all been able to build because of the amazing foundation she fought for and sacrificed to lay for us…one painstaking example laid upon another.

I remember a conversation with my *Yia'Yia'* after our final trip to Greece in 2007, after so many great stories had been told. She said to me, *"You should write a book about them."* I agreed wholeheartedly, but every time I tried to write, life seemed to interrupt. I couldn't get started. She prodded me about the book on several occasions when we would meet. Then one day she said with her usual candor, "Well, I probably won't get to read it before I die."

"You probably won't," I confessed, "but I *promise* you, I will write it…I'll call it 'Shortie'." That coaxed a chuckle from her as it always did. It pains me that I didn't get this book written in time for her to read it. She deserved to have her perseverance and accomplishments recorded and acknowledged. She deserved to hear the impact she has had on all of us. But I console myself, hoping she already knew.

It has been a privilege to sift through the facts, dates and stories of her life. Each time I relive a memory, it is like spending time with her…like enjoying one of our many *bacon-sandwich-Pepsi and-potato-chip* lunches together on TV trays in her wood paneled family room. Maybe I had trouble sitting down to write because I subconsciously didn't want our time together to end.

It was a bittersweet day when the writing for this book was complete; as if I had to say a final goodbye. But she will always remain in our hearts, our memories and the way we continue to live our lives. If I could write her a letter, I would say…

My Dearest Shortie!

I'm sorry you had to wait so long. But I finally kept my promise. I finished your book! The next time I return to Toledo, I will go to the cemetery and visit your grave. I'll trim the weeds, bring a pretty, flowering plant, burn some incense and read This book out loud to you, and to all the relatives who passed before or after you, so they can finally hear *your* story. I know I said I'd title it "*Shortie*", but I thought the letters of your name that you wrote on your immigration papers were somehow more appropriate; *Twenty simple letters, perfectly formed* that transformed a brave little girl into a strong and resilient young woman who sacrificed and laid an invaluable foundation for our entire family, so we could attain *our* dreams. Thank you, Shortie. I Love you with all my heart!

Your Granddaughter,
Karen

Moments after I typed those final words at my usual coffee shop, there was an ear-splitting sound of seemingly every metal pan in the kitchen clattering loudly to the floor. The act was punctuated by another caffeinated patron good-humoredly shouting *"OPA!"* I thought it couldn't have been a more fitting end point to this book. I viewed it as a sign that you were celebrating its completion with me!

OPA!
AN EXPRESSION OF HAPPINESS THAT IS
FREQUENTLY UTTERED DURING GREEK
CELEBRATIONS AND DANCING,. OFTEN
ACCENTUATED WITH THE SMASHING OF PLATES.

ATHANASOULI FAMILY RECIPES

The following are recipes for most of the Greek food mentioned in this book as well as other family favorites. We hope you share them with people you love and find them as delicious, comforting and sustaining as they have been for our family.

TIRO TRIGONA

(Filo Wrapped Cheese Puff Triangles)

4 eggs, well beaten
1 - 8 oz. pkg. cream cheese
1 lb. feta cheese
1 lb. filo dough
1.2 lb. butter, melted

Beat the eggs until fluffy and blend in the cream cheese. Crumble the Feta cheese with a fork and add to the egg mixture, blending thoroughly. Place one sheet of filo on the work surface, brush with melted butter. Place another sheet of filo on top and brush with melted butter again. Working along the length of the sheet, figure six to nine strips along the short length, score with a knife and place a spoonful of mixture on each strip, about an inch in from the edge. Now pick-up the corner and bring it to the opposite side to form a triangle, and keep picking-up the back corner and laying over to the other side, forming triangles as you go (like folding a flag). Tuck ends underneath. Brush the top with butter. Lay the tiropita on a greased baking sheet, at least 1" apart and bake at 375 degrees for about 20 minutes, or until the tops are golden.

May be frozen. Can be baked frozen.

Yield: Approximately 90 pieces

SPANAKOPITA

(Spinach and Feta cheese baked in filo)

2 pkgs. frozen chopped spinach (if using fresh spinach, chop and
heat to wilt and pour off residual liquid).
1 lb. butter melted
1 bunch green onions
1 lb. filo dough
1 lb. Feta cheese crumbled
Salt and pepper
7 eggs
¼ cup chopped parsley
1 Tbsp. fresh mint leaves

Thaw spinach and squeeze out moisture. Melt butter and chop onions,
parsley and Feta Cheese. Place six pastry sheets in a greased 9x13
Pyrex pan, spreading each with melted butter. Mix all ingredients
and add unbeaten eggs and mix well. Spread into pan. Cover with
six buttered pastry sheets (brushed individually with melted butter).
Lightly score the top of the filo into squares. Bake at 350 degrees for
one hour. After baking for 30 minutes, pour remaining melted butter
over the top of the pita. Finish baking. Cool for twenty minutes and
cut into squares.

Yield: 20

DOLMADES

(STUFFED GRAPE LEAVES)

1 jar grapevine leaves (1 pint)
1/4 cup fresh mint
1½ lbs. ground beef
2 tsp. Salt
1 large onion grated
Pepper to taste
1 egg
2 Tbsp. Vegetable oil
½ cup rice (long-grained)
2 cups chicken broth or water
½ cup chopped parsley
¼ cup butter

Remove the grapevine leaves from the jar. Wash leaves thoroughly and drain, then with a sharp knife, cut the heavy stems from the leaves. (If using fresh grapevine leaves, use the same procedure, par boiling leaves, if not tender, for 5 minutes, then drain.) Line a medium, high-sided pot with a few heavy grapevine leaves and set aside. Combine ground meat with all the ingredients except the chicken broth, adding 3/4 cup of warm water to make a soft loose mixture. To stuff a grapevine leaf, put it on your working surface, rough side up and stem end near you, and place a teaspoon of the meat mixture near the stem end. Using both hands, fold the part of the leaf near you up and over the filling, then the left side and shape into a narrow roll. Place the arranged dolma, seam side down, in the prepared pan and arrange dolmades in layers. Add chicken broth or water, butter and salt and cover with an inverted plate (to prevent them from moving while boiling). Bring to a boil, then cover and simmer for about 45 minutes or longer if needed. Serve hot with egg-lemon sauce.

Yield: About 65 small rolls.

(EGG-LEMON SAUCE FOR DOLMADES)

4 eggs
3 Tbsp. Water
Juice of 2 lemons
Broth from dolmades

In a mixing bowl, beat eggs until light and fluffy, add lemon juice and water, blending well. Gradually add hot liquid (from dolmades), a little at a time, beating constantly to temper. Remove the saucepan from heat, pour egg sauce slowly over the dolmades. Shake the saucepan to spread the sauce evenly. Serve at once.

FASOLÁKIA YIACHNI

(Stewed Green Beans)

1 lb. Green Beans
1 large can diced Tomatoes
2 onions, chopped
1 clove garlic, chopped
¼ cup olive oil
salt, pepper to taste

Sauté onions and garlic in oil. Add tomatoes, bring to a boil and add beans. Season to taste. Cook until the beans are tender. Cut up potatoes and carrots can be added if desired.

Yield: 6-8 servings

MANESTRA

(Orzo with Chicken Broth & Tomato)

2 cups uncooked Orzo pasta
3 cups chicken broth
½ - ¾ cups tomato sauce
⅓ cup butter or drippings from a baked chicken

Bring chicken broth to a boil. Add Orzo, butter and/or chicken drippings. Boil until orzo reaches the ' el dente' stage. Add tomato sauce (enough to give it a rich orange color). Continue to boil on low until cooked.

8 servings (1/2 cup each)

PSOME

(New Year's Bread With Silver Coin Baked Inside)

1 cup butter
½ cup potato water (in which potatoes boiled, cooled to lukewarm)
6 large eggs
1½ cups sugar
2 pkgs. dry yeast
½ cup cinnamon water (1 cup water boiled w/ 2-3 sticks cinnamon
   for 5 mins., and cooled). Cinnamon sticks are optional.
1 tsp. salt
1 egg yolk, mixed with 1 Tbsp. Water
2 ½ lbs. all-purpose flour
½ tsp. Baking powder
2 medium white potatoes (boiled and mashed)
Sesame seeds
1 silver coin (washed and wrapped in foil)

Heat oven to 350 degrees and grease four 9-inch cake pans. Beat butter until white and fluffy, add sugar, beat well, add eggs and beat again. Dissolve yeast in the potato water. It takes about 5 minutes for the yeast to dissolve and it appears rather foamy. Add the yeast mixture to the butter mixture and mix well. Add the cinnamon water and mix well. Then add the mashed potatoes and mix well. Add the flour and baking powder and mix well. More flour may be necessary. Knead for about 15 minutes. Wash a silver coin and work into the dough. Place dough in a greased bowl or large kettle, cover with a damp towel and put in a warm place to let rise until doubled in size. Punch down and let rise a second time. Punch down again and divide into 4 loaves and place into the greased pans, return it to warm area until doubled in size. Brush tops with the egg yolk mixture and add sesame seeds if you wish. Bake for about 1 hour or until the tops are a deep golden brown. Remove from pans immediately and cool loaves on cake racks.

Note: Slice bread starting with one for "The House" followed by each member of the family from oldest to youngest. The person whose slice hits the silver coin, is promised good luck in the new year.

PATATO SALATA

(Warm Greek Potato Salad)

7 potatoes
1 large onion
⅓ cup olive oil
½ cup vinegar
1 lemon (squeezed)
Salt and pepper to taste
Parsley

Boil potatoes until tender. Peel potatoes (optional), slice into quarters. Place in a bowl. Add salt and pepper to taste and remaining ingredients. Toss lightly and serve warm.

Yield: 7-8 servings

SPANAKORIZO

(Spinach with Rice and tomato)

1 lb. spinach
2 medium onions, coarsely chopped
1 Tbsp. chopped dill
1 cup rice
1 cup tomato sauce
¼ cup oil
Salt and pepper

Sauté onions in hot olive oil and add the spinach which has been washed and drained. Add 2 cups of water, one cup of tomato sauce and bring to a boil. Sprinkle in the dill and add the rice. Stir thoroughly, season, cover and simmer for 25 minutes. Add more tomato sauce as needed.

Yield: 4-6 servings

AVGOLEMONO SOUPA

(Egg Lemon Soup)

1 qt chicken broth
1 cup orzo
2 eggs, separated
½ cup lemon juice
Salt to taste

Cook orzo in broth. Beat egg whites till fluffy, add yolks and beat to combine. Mix in lemon juice. Slowly pour enough broth into egg mixture, stirring continuously to warm it. Pour into remaining soup. Salt to taste.

Yield - 6 servings.

MAGYAR ITZA

GREEK EASTER SOUP
(Avgolemono Soup With Ground Lamb or Beef)

Heart, liver, lungs and intestines of young lamb (substitute 1-2 lbs.
    ground lamb or beef)
2 qt. beef broth
½ cup butter
4 bunches green onions, chopped
¼ cup fresh dill, minced
¼ cup fresh parsley, minced
2 tsp. salt
½ tsp. pepper
⅓ cup long-grain rice
4 eggs, separated
Juice of 2 lemons
1 Tbsp. tomato paste

Melt butter and brown ground meat and saute chopped onions and herbs. Add seasonings and tomato paste. Simmer until onions are tender. Add 2 qts. Beef broth and rice, cover and simmer for 20 minutes. Remove from heat.

Avgolemono Sauce: Beat egg whites until stiff. Continue beating and add yolks, one at a time. While beating, add lemon juice and several cups of broth "a little at a time" to avoid curdling. Pour the mixture back into the pot, stirring well over very low heat until thickened. Do not boil, as it will curdle.

Yield: 8-9 servings

PASTICHIO

(Pasta with ground beef casserole with white sauce)

1 lb. ground beef
1 tsp. dried mint, chopped fine
1 tsp. salt
¼ cup Mazola or vegetable oil
1 medium onion chopped
6 Tbsp dry wine
¼ tsp. black pepper
¾ cup tomato sauce (small can)
⅛ tsp. nutmeg
½ tsp. Sugar
⅛ tsp. cinnamon
Few sprigs parsley, chopped finely

Sauté onion for 2-3 minutes in oil. Add meat and brown lightly over moderate flame for another 8-10 minutes. Add all other ingredients and continue cooking for 5-6 minutes.

½ lb. macaroni
⅛ tsp. black pepper
¼ cup melted butter
4 Tbsp. grated Romano cheese
1½ tsp. salt
2 beaten eggs

Boil macaroni in unsalted water until almost done. Rinse well in hot water, and allow it to drain well in the sieve. Put in a large bowl, add salt, black pepper, melted butter and cheese. Then add the beaten eggs and mix lightly.

(White Sauce)

½ cup butter, melted
1½ tsp. Salt
½ cup bread flour

3 large, or 4 small eggs, beaten well
3 cups warm milk
¼ cup grated romano cheese

Place butter in a large saucepan over moderate flame until it begins to turn light brown only. Add flour and stir until smooth. Add 3 cups milk, a little at a time, stirring constantly to make a smooth sauce. Add salt and cook until thick; simmer for a few minutes. Just before the simmering point, add the cheese. Allow the sauce to cool.

When the sauce has cooled, add gradually to the beaten eggs (to temper). Beat eggs in a large bowl in order to keep beating while adding the white sauce.

Mix macaroni and meat mixture and about one-third of the white sauce. Pour into an oblong buttered baking pan about 13"x9"x9". Sprinkle top with a little grated cheese and bake in a preheated oven at 350 degrees for about 15 minutes.

Remove from the oven and pour the remaining white sauce over partially-baked macaroni. Sprinkle a little more cheese on top. Continue baking for about another 30 minutes, or until a medium-brown color has been achieved. Remove from the oven and cool on a rack. Allow Pasticho to stand at least 3-45 minutes before cutting into squares.

Yield: 12 medium servings.

Note: To make the very large pan of Pasticho, this recipe must be tripled. Use a little less than the full 1 ½ lbs. of macaroni. 2 ½ lbs. of meat are also adequate.

ARNI PSITO

(Roast Leg Of Lamb)

5 lb. leg of lamb
3 cloves of garlic, slivered
2 tsp. Salt
1 tsp. Pepper
2 Tbsp oregano
1 lemon
¼ cup butter
¼ cup olive oil
1 cup water

Wash meat well and set on a rack in a roasting pan. Mix slivered cloves of garlic, salt, pepper and oregano. Make incisions in the leg of lamb with a sharp knife and insert the seasoned slivers of garlic which have been dipped in the olive oil and melted butter mixture. Sprinkle the rest of the meat with salt, pepper and oregano. Rub the remaining mixture of butter and olive oil all over the surface of the lamb. Pour the juice of one lemon over it. Cover the roasting pan and cook at 325 degrees for 3 hours. During the roasting period, add one cup of water to the liquid in the pan and baste often until the meat is browned and done to the taste. Half way through the cooking period, small peeled potatoes or small onions may be placed in the roasting pan around the lamb.

Yield: 10 generous servings

MOUSSAKA

(Eggplant casserole)

2 eggplants (med. size)
2 eggs - separated
1 ½ lbs. ground beef
2 Tbsp. Chopped parsley
2 medium onions finely chopped
¼ cup grated Parmesan cheese
5 Tbsp. Bread crumbs
Salt & pepper to taste
1 Tbsp. Tomato paste
2 Tbsp. Butter or olive oil
½ cup dry white wine

Brown the meat with the butter, adding the 2 onions. When both are golden brown, add the wine, tomato paste, parsley and salt and pepper to taste. If the mixture seems too dry, add a little tomato juice and let simmer for about 45 minutes or until very little moisture remains. Cut eggplants into ¼ inch round slices and fry in a little vegetable oil or brush both sides with oil and broil eggplants until golden brown on both sides.

Butter a casserole dish and sprinkle the bottom with ½ of bread crumbs. Then put in a layer of eggplant. Now add 3 tablespoons of breadcrumbs to the meat mixture and 2 egg whites. Mix everything well. Then put a layer of the meat on the layer of eggplant, sprinkle with a liberal amount of grated Parmesan cheese and top with the remaining eggplant and beef.

Sauce:
4 ½ - 5 cups warm milk
8 Tbs. butter
4 Tbs. flour
Dash nutmeg
Salt to taste

In the meantime, prepare the sauce. Melt Butter in the pan, add flour, stirring constantly. Add warm milk and keep stirring until it thickens, is smooth and free of lumps. Add salt and nutmeg.

Remove from heat and mix spoonfuls of milk mixture slowly into 2 well-beaten eggs to temper them before adding the rest of the milk mixture (to avoid curdling the eggs). Pour this sauce over the eggplant and meat casserole, sprinkle with more grated Parmesan cheese and bread crumbs, dot with butter and bake in a moderate oven for 45 minutes uncovered. When finished, the top should be a golden brown.

Yield: 10-12 servings

YEMISTA

(Green Peppers and/or Tomatoes Stuffed
With Hamburger and Rice)

14 medium, green peppers
2 Tbsp. Chopped parsley
2 lbs. lean ground beef
6 Tbsp. Butter
3 medium onions chopped fine
1 tsp. Cinnamon
½ cup tomato sauce
2 tsp. Salt or more to taste
Dash of pepper
2 Tbsp. Dried mint
¾ cup long-grain rice
1 Clove garlic, minced

Wash peppers, remove seeds. Cut-off tops of peppers w/ stems carefully, saving tops for covers. Sauté ground beef with butter in a skillet for 5 minutes. Add rice, and parsley and fry for about 2 minutes, stirring constantly. Add cinnamon, salt and pepper to taste. Add tomato sauce and water and simmer until some of the liquid is absorbed (mixture should have some liquid so that rice can cook).

Fill peppers with meat mixture, cover with stem end of pepper, and place in a baking pan with 1 1/2 cups of water, 1 cup of tomato sauce and pieces of butter. Bake in an oven at 350 degrees for about 1 hour and 20 minutes. Baste peppers occasionally with pan juices.

Stuffed Tomatoes - Remove a thin slice from the tops of the tomatoes, scoop out pulp, and add to the meat mixture. Simmer with meat and rice. Stuff tomatoes and bake as directed above.

Yield: 7-8 servings.

GALATOBOUREKO

(Farina Custard Pastry)

8 cups milk
½ lb. package of filo pastry sheets
6 eggs
1 lb. sweet butter (unsalted, melted)
1 ½ cups sugar
1 ½ Tbsp. Vanilla
1 cup farina (cream of wheat)
Sugar syrup (see below)

Heat milk slowly, bring to scalding, then add farina, stirring constantly and bring to boil. Separate eggs and beat the egg whites until very stiff. Beat yolks for several minutes until they are light, then fold into egg whites. Fold the egg mixture into the farina and cook until very thick. Remove from heat and add the vanilla and cool. Butter the bottom and sides of a 9"x13"x2 1/2" pan. Place half of the filo sheets on the bottom of the baking pan, buttering each sheet of filo as you build, being careful to bring edges of pastry up sides of pan to turn back later over custard filling. Pour the cooled farina mixture over the filo. Add the other half of the file sheets on top, again buttering each sheet of filo. Fold in the edges. Brush top with melted butter. Bake for 1 hour in a 350-degree oven until the top is golden brown. Cut into Diamond shapes and pour very cool syrup over the hot Galaktoboureko.

Sugar Syrup:
3 cups sugar
2 cups water
1 cinnamon stick
1 oz. brandy

Mix sugar, water and cinnamon stick in a saucepan and bring to a boil. Boil gently until the syrup is thickened, about 20-30 minutes. Remove cinnamon stick and add brandy. Be sure to cool completely. Before pouring over the Galaktoboureko. The syrup can be made a day or two before.

Yield: 15 servings

LOUKOUMADES

(Greek Doughnuts)

2 pkgs. yeast
1 cup warm water
⅓ cup warm water
1 qt. oil for frying
2 cups flour
2 cups honey
1 tsp. Sugar
1 cup water
¼ tsp salt
Ground cinnamon

Dissolve yeast in warm water. Put dry ingredients in a bowl, adding warm water and yeast mixture. Mix well by hand. Soft dough will form. (Add more flour if necessary). Cover and set aside in a warm place for dough to rise, about 2 hours. Heat oil in a deep pan. Drop a teaspoon of batter in hot oil. Fry until golden brown. Using a slotted spoon, remove from oil. Drain on absorbent paper. Heat honey and water. Dip each doughnut into the mixture. Remove. Sprinkle with cinnamon. Serve hot. Can also roll hot, drained dough in cinnamon sugar or powdered sugar instead of honey mixture.

Yield: 30

DIPLES

(Fried Pastry Rosettes Drizzled With Honey, Cinnamon & Walnuts)

3 eggs. Beat until foamy
1 Tbsp. Oil
2 ½ to 3 cups flour - Soft enough to roll out
1 jigger of cognac
1 jar honey

Beat eggs until lemon-colored. Add oil and cognac. Sift together dry ingredients. Add about 2/3 to the egg mixture and beat well. Working the rest of the flour by hand until the dough is soft and does not stick to fingers. Knead dough until it is soft and smooth and separate into four parts. Cover with plastic wrap and let rest for 3 hours on the counter. Roll each part on a floured board with a long, thin dowel until it is paper thin. Using a pastry wheel, cut 2" strips and about 4" long. Drop strip into deep, hot oil at 356 degrees. Using two forks, turn dough over <u>immediately</u> and roll quickly, jelly-roll fashion, before it becomes crisp. Fry until it holds shape and becomes very light brown. Drain and place on absorbent paper. Dilute honey with a little warm water and drizzle over diples. Sprinkle tops with a mixture of cinnamon and very finely chopped walnuts. (Gorgeous, like delicate rosette sculptures).

Yield: about 40

KOURAMBIETHES

(Short, powdered sugar covered cookies)

1 lb. sweet butter
1 large egg
¼ cup powdered sugar
½ cup orange juice
2 oz of whiskey
½ tsp. Baking powder
1 cup ground walnuts
5-6 cups flour (until dough holds together)

Beat butter until very fluffy. Add Egg, whiskey, orange juice and ¼ cup powdered sugar. Mix well. Sift cake flour with baking powder. Add to egg/butter mixture and mix well. Roll dough into round balls, the diameter of a half dollar. Flatten out in Palm of your hand, add 1/2 tsp. Ground walnuts. Fold over and roll in your hand to 1 1/2 inches in length or round ball. Bake 300 degrees for 15-20 minutes

Place close together on a clean newspaper. While still hot, sift powdered sugar over them until buried completely on all sides. When cooled, place in small individual cupcake papers.

Yield: Approximately 50 pieces

KOULOURAKIA

(Butter Cookies)

1 lb. butter
2 cups sugar
5 tsp. baking powder
4 whole eggs <u>and</u> 4 egg yolks
4 - 5 cups flour
Sesame seeds

Cream butter, add sugar and beat thoroughly. Add beaten eggs and yolks one at a time. Sift together dry ingredients and add gradually to the butter mixture. Last cup or so must be mixed by hand, as the dough should be stiff enough to shape by hand. Roll a rounded Tbsp of dough by hand into a 6-inch long "rope" approximately ½" in diameter, then shape into cookies: doubled-in-half rope twist, concentric circle or "S"-shaped swirl. Brush tops of cookies with a mixture of slightly beaten egg yolk and teaspoon of water and sprinkle with sesame seeds. (optional). Bake in a 350 degree oven for about 20-25 minutes until golden brown on the bottoms. Do not brown tops.

Yield: About six dozen cookies.

AUTHOR BIOGRAPHY

Karen S. Barbera is a Public Relations professional who has worked with some of the top consumer product companies, including Wendy's, Kraft Foods, Procter & Gamble, Avon Products, The Campbell Soup Company, Dial, Abbott Laboratories, Junior Achievement and The Ford Motor Company.

She has authored three additional books on historically significant individuals, contributed to several magazines and conducted investigative journalism for *The Wall Street Journal,* Ohio's Bureau of Criminal Investigations, KVOA-TV (NBC) and the Arizona Attorney General.

Karen S. Barbera and her husband Randy reside in Southern California and enjoy spending time with their six grown children and their expanding families.

ADDITIONAL BOOKS

By Karen S. Barbera

"Bouquets of Brushes, Patches of Paint -
The Art of Pauline Roche"

"10,000 Feet & Climbing -
The Aviation Adventures of
Richard E. Schreder"

"Duke Ellington - The Notes
The World Was Not Ready
To Hear"

www.ingramcontent.com/pod-product-compliance
Lightning Source LLC
Chambersburg PA
CBHW050520160726
48003CB00001B/393